Foreword

D0619310

Since the Sustainable Buildings Industry Council (SBIC) started working on the initial version of the *Green Building Guidelines: Meeting the Demand for Low-Energy, Resource-Efficient Homes* in 2000, much has changed. Nearly two million housing units have have been built every year. The impact of all of this construction has been positive as it rippled through the economy, helping to keep it stronger longer than could have been predicted.

There has also been a down side. Consider these facts: every year constructing and operating America's buildings generates about 25% of the total municipal solid waste stream and 48% of all greenhouse gas emissions. The industry uses over 25% of the total amount of water, and a whopping 76% of the electricity generated in the US. And our country's insatiable appetite for energy to power these new homes keeps increasing, which results in more and more air pollution. An unprecedented number of natural disasters, wildfires, tornadoes, and most notably Hurricane Katrina, have damaged or destroyed hundreds of thousands of homes, many of which still await final demolition before being taken off to the landfill.

During the same six year period, the green phenomenon has taken firm hold nationally, touching many aspects of our lives: from everyday purchases such as organic foods and hybrid cars to the more heady concept proposed by economists and environmentalists to quantify the US green Gross Domestic Product. Green magazines and e-newsletters are springing up everywhere. Coverage in top national newspapers such as *The New York Times*, the *LA Times*, and *The Washington Post* is regular and in-depth. Cover stories and entire issues devoted to green are found in *Time, Newsweek, CNN Money, Vanity Fair*, and *Good Housekeeping*.

The construction and home building sectors are no exception. The green home building movement, which applies environmentally sensitive design and construction techniques to reduce energy and water consumption and improve residential comfort and safety, has moved rapidly into the mainstream. By 2005, the National Association of Home Builders (NAHB) had already held its fourth annual green building conference called "Greening the American Dream." That same year, NAHB published the *Model Green Home Building Guidelines* and the accompanying *Green Home Building Checklist* designed as a tool kit for local associations that wanted to create their own customized green home building programs. NAHB's goal to move environmentally-friendly home building concepts further into the mainstream marketplace continues to be a high priority in 2007.

The U.S. Green Building Council (USGBC) also launched a residential program and is now pilot testing *LEED® for Homes* (LEED-H). This voluntary rating system, targeted to reach the top 25% of homes with best practices and environmental features, is expected to be formally released in late 2007. It is just one part of the suite of assessment tools offered by the USGBC.

At last count, more than 60 local green building programs had been established by homebuilder associations, utilities, local governments and nonprofit groups across the U.S., and there are many more ready to launch.

Continued growth in the marketplace for green/sustainable homes is being predicted. Results from the *McGraw-Hill Key Trends/SmartMarket Report* published in 2006, found a 20% increase in 2005 in the members of the home building community who were focusing more attention on environmentally responsible building. That number was expected to increase by another 30% in 2006. The study showed that after several years of slow but steady growth across the country, by 2010, the residential green building business might grow as high as $38 billion.

With such a dynamic landscape, an update of the *Green Building Guidelines* was warranted. In addition to educating newcomers to green home build-ing, we are eager to share SBIC's overarching philosphy that sustainability, while critcial, cannot stand alone. A more inclusive "whole building approach" is required and is summarized for readers of this new edition.

How to Use this Book

SBIC's *Green Buildilng Guildelines* was the first national green home building resource written by builders for builders. While it is still primarily a builder's guide, the information will be valuable to anyone who wants to learn more about the various aspects that make up green home design. For example, homeowners may find it a valuable resource when working with a builder. The Table of Contents is organized by the Sustainability Principles (optimize site design, save energy and water, improve indoor environmental quality, use green products and systems, and optimize O&M). You will also find a Builder's Matrix, organized by the stages of a project (land development, construction waste management, foundations, framing, exterior finishing, HVAC, interior finishing, landscaping, etc.).

The text has been organized to acquaint the reader with basic concepts and provides resources that offer more detailed information. At the end of each section, you will find "Interactions," which are references to other sections of the book describing design strategies, systems, components, or materials that may interact in important ways with the topic of the chapter.

SBIC recognizes that there are many shades of green. Whether or not the strategies and materials you select are cost-effective, practical, and attractive enough to offer you a significant market advantage over your competitors depends on specific local factors such as costs, climate, and market characteristics. Just how green to be is a decision made by builders, often with their clients, during the design and development stages of each project. The Fifth Edition of the *Green Building Guidelines* should also be a particularly helpful tool in discussions with your subcontractors, suppliers, developers, and business partners.

History of the Green Building Guidelines

In 1998, with support from the U.S. Department of Energy's Office of Building Technology and its *Building America Program* partners at the Consortium for Advanced Residential Building (CARB) managed by Steven Winter Associates, Inc., SBIC formed a committee of builders (both members and non-members of NAHB, architects, building scientists, product suppliers and manufacturers and others, and set out to develop guidelines for builders who were interested in environmentally friendly design and construction. The result was the First Edition of SBIC's *Green Building Guidelines*, published in 2000. The Committee pulled together research, information, tips and resources into a single builder-friendly document that had previously been scattered across more than 100 different books, videos, and Web sites. Since its first printing more than 5,000 copies have been disseminated nationwide.

Acknowledgments

Special thanks are due to the following individuals and organizations whose assistance during various phases of the project was invaluable.

Early conceptual design:
  Helen English, SBIC, *David Johnston*, What's Working

Advisory Committee and Contributors:
  Steve Ashkin, Ashkin Group, LLC, *Michael Bell*, The Bell Company, *Perry Bigelow*, Bigelow Homes, *Eric Borsting*, ConSol Energy Consultants, *Koben Calhoun*, Built Green™, *Charles Cottrell*, North American Insulation Manu-facturers Association, *Rich Dooley*, NAHB Research Center, *William Eich*, Bill Eich Construction Co., Inc., *Tom Farkas*, Edison Electric Institute, *Judy Fosdick*, Tierra Concrete Homes, Inc., *Jay Hall*, USGBC, *Bruce Harley*, Conservation Services Group, *Bion Howard*, Building Environmental Science and Technology, *Ronald Jones*, Sierra Custom Builders, *Michael Kirkbride*, Kirkbride Homes, *Lee Kitson*, Lee Kitson Builder, Inc., *Mark Magrann*, Magrann Associates, *Doug Parker*, Big Horn Builders, Inc., *William Reed*, Natural Logic, *Henry Rogers*, Turtle Logic, *John Sullivan*, Portland Cement Association, *Ray Tonjes*, Ray Tonjes Builder, Inc., *Brian Trimble*, Brick Industry Association, *Martha VanGeem*, CTLGroup (for PCA), Michael Virga, American Forest & Paper Association, *D'Lane Wisner*, APC, *Alex Wilson*, BuildingGreen, Inc.

Content for the *Green Building Guidelines* was derived from numerous existing resources, primarily SBIC's *Passive Solar Design Strategies: Guide-lines for Home Building*. Extensive information and graphics were pulled from the NAHB Research Center's *A Guide to Developing Green Builder Programs* and Georgia Environmental Facilities Authority's *A Builder's Guide to Energy Efficient Homes in Georgia*. Content was also extracted from many publicly funded Web sites (U.S. Department of Energy, California Energy Commission, etc.) and the following publications:

Designing Low-Energy Buildings with Energy-10, SBIC
E Seal Certification Manual, Edison Electric Institute
Green Building Advisor, BuildingGreen, Inc.
GreenSpec, BuildingGreen, Inc.
Guide to Resource Efficient Building Elements, National Center for
    Appropriate Technology
Guidelines for Uniformity: Voluntary Procedures for Home Energy Ratings,
    Home Energy Rating Systems (HERS) Council
High Performance Building Guidelines, City of New York Department of
    Design and Construction
Sustainable Building Technical Manual, U.S. Green Building Council
Super Good Cents Builder's Field Guide, Bonneville Power Administration

Sustainable Buildings Industry Council:
    Helen English, Executive Director
    Douglas Hargrave, Project Coordinator
    Doug Schroeder, Associate Director
    Cynthia Gardstein, Fifth Edition Editing and Design
    Josephine Mooney, Fifth Edition Production

Thanks also to Bambi Tran, Dianne Griffiths, John Amatruda, Ric Guilbert,
Gordon Tully, and other Steven Winter Associates, Inc., personnel who
contributed as part of the U.S. DOE's Building America research program.

About SBIC

To fulfill its mission to unite and inspire the building industry toward higher performing buildings, SBIC conducts on education, outreach and advocacy activities. Since its founding in 1980, the Council has produced dozens of targeted educational resources for building industry professionals, such as the *Green Building Guidelines* book and workshop series, the *High Performance School Buildings Resource and Strategy Guide*, online sustainability training courses, and *Energy-10*™ – a energy simulation tool for small commercial buildings and homes.

As we present the Fifth Edition of the *Green Building Guidelines*, the Sustainable Buildings Industry Council salutes the thousands of home builders who have adopted green building practices to create comfortable, beautiful, and resource-efficient homes since the Guidelines were first published.

Contents

Builder's Matrix

	1. Community and Site Planning	2. Renewable Energy	3. The Building Envelope	4. Energy Efficiency	5. Efficient Water Use	6. Indoor Environmental Quality	7. Materials	8. Operation and Maintenance
Land Development	1-8	19-29						
Site Planning	1, 3, 4, 5, 9-13	10,19-29, 35		2, 7, 10,76	90-96	99	120, 126	
Construction Waste Management	14-18		44				109, 110,	
Renewable Energy (Passive Solar/PV)	1-2, 10-12	19-40	53	76-77	30-33	105	118, 126-128	
Foundations			41-43, 50,			99	112-113, 120	
Framing		35	43-44				113-114, 121, 125	
Exterior Finishing		19-24	43, 45-46				115-119	115
Roofing		30-33, 34-36	43, 45				116	
Plumbing	4	30-33	43, 50-51	72-74, 80-82	84-96	106		
HVAC		19	43, 46, 48, 49, 50-55, 59-73	57-71	64	97-103,	116, 126	127
Electrical		34-40	50-52	76-84	86	105		
Windows		19-25	48, 49, 50-56	21-25, 53		103	118, 126-127	
Insulation and Air Leakage		28-29	46-49, 50-55, 118	117-119		99	116-117	
Interior Finishes		25-26	43, 48, 50-55			105	119-120	1
Flooring		25-26	43, 48, 50-55			104-105	119-120	127
Landscaping	4-5, 9-13	20, 21, 23, 24	45, 78, 79	77	90-94			139

Understanding Green & the Whole Building Approach

Principles of Green Design

The precise definition of exactly what is and isn't a green home is still a moving target. A broad array of programs, rating systems, and laws define requirements differently, causing spirited debate nationwide.

The *Green Building Guidelines* covers six overarching and interrelated principles, noted below, but does not attempt to assign point values to the individual strategies. We've left that to the rating programs.

Optimize Site Potential. This principle covers such aspects as proper site selection, consideration of any existing buildings or infrastructure, orientation of streets and homes for passive and active solar features, location of access roads, parking, potential hazards, and any high priority resources which should be conserved such as trees, waterways, snags, and animal habitats.

Minimize Energy Use and Use Renewable Energy Strategies. This principle covers aspects such as the importance of dramatically reducing the overall energy loads (through insulation, efficient equipment and lighting, and careful detailing of the entire envelope), limiting the amount of fossil fuels required, incorporating renewable energy systems such as photovoltaics, geothermal heat pumps and solar water heating whenever feasible, and purchasing of green power in order to minimize the creation of greenhouse gasses.

Conserve and Protect Water. This principle covers aspects such as reducing, controlling or treating site runoff; designing and constructing the home to conserve water used inside and outside; and minimizing leaks by insuring proper inspections during construction.

Use Environmentally Preferable Products. This principle covers such aspects as specifying products which are salvaged, made with recycled content, conserve natural resources, reduce overall material use, are exceptionally durable or low maintenance, naturally or minimally processed, save energy and/or water, and/or reduce pollution or waste from operations.

Enhance Indoor Environmental Quality. This principle covers strategies to provide excellent acoustical, thermal and visual qualities which have a significant impact on health, comfort, and productivity. Other attributes to be considered: maximized daylight, appropriate ventilation and moisture control, and the use of low- or no VOC products.

Optimize Operations and Maintenance Practices. This principle covers materials and systems that simplify and reduce operational requirements; require less water, energy, and toxic chemicals and cleaners to maintain; are cost-effective and reduce life-cycle costs.

When to Apply Green Building Strategies

It is very important that each green building strategy be applied at the appropriate stage to avoid closing off options. For example, not much can be done to affect the orientation of the house after the framing is underway, but much can be done during the *design* of the home, and even more during the layout of roads and lots. The chart below gives a rough guide for when to consider major design issues, systems, and components.

Appropriate Stage of Design and Construction to Apply Green Building Strategies

Stage	Issues to Consider	
Land Planning	Solar access Transportation Greyfield / brownfield / infill Saving natural plants and areas Mixed use Reduced paving Infrastructure	Clustering Community stormwater management Wind buffers Wildfire buffers Buffers from undesirable adjacent development Traditional Neighborhood Development Utilities
Site Planning	Wind buffers Porches and decks Reduced site paving Grading and site water management Landscaping and shading Acoustical and visual buffers	Basic space layout in home relative to sun (for initial solar access design), wind, and views Septic systems and wells Utility service entries Auto and pedestrian access Parking
Construction Process Planning	Construction waste management and recycling Hazardous waste disposal	Reduced site disturbance Site construction access and storage Storage and reuse of on-site excavation & soils
Basic Design	Glazing and solar access Provisions for efficient and energy-saving duct layout Mechanical equipment inside the conditioned envelope Acoustical considerations	Design for recycling for homeowners Avoiding attached garage if possible Avoiding excessive size Incorporate natural lighting wherever possible Structural systems
Specifications	**Green your specs:** Structural materials Cladding and roofing Insulation Air-sealing materials and systems Finish materials	Cabinetwork and accessories Plumbing and water heating Mechanical equipment selection Electrical and lighting
During Construction	Changes that do not affect other elements and do not increase energy consumption or otherwise compromise green building standards	Photograph and record work that will be hidden
Post-construction	"Commission" to ensure proper operation of green building elements and systems	"Commissioning" mechanical & other systems Home Energy Rating/ENERGY STAR® approval Home buyer education and operating manual

Different Names for Green

Various terms are used to describe green design, including sustainable and environmentally responsive. Industry leaders are beginning to articulate the differences among these terms and the more comprehensive high performance design, which relies on the whole building approach.

An Integrated Approach

It is all too common to focus on one aspect of the house and ignore other important elements. For example, designing an air-tight, well-insulated wall system and then choosing low-quality windows which are then poorly installed results in energy loss, higher costs, and owner discomfort. The whole building approach encourages balance among the necessary measures. Many green building programs help foster this balance by requiring mandatory attention to all six green principles covered above, and not just one area, such as selecting sustainable, healthy materials.

Accessing Local Green Building Programs

The expanded market interest in green homes has driven an increase in the number of green building programs across the country. In general, local green home building programs offer building professionals and home owners a localized system to measure or rate the greenness of a home building project. These programs also provide valuable information on the benefits of green building and of buying green-built homes. Some local programs offer resources and incentives to build green, and provide training to help home builders design and construct green homes. See the section on Green Building Programs near the end of this book for contact information.

The Importance of Energy

One prevalent myth is that it is possible to make a home green simply by using green products or adding some energy-conserving measures, equipment or appliances. While not bad in themselves, such improvements miss the point that a higher performing home will only result when all aspects are considered on an equal footing. Token measures also give a false sense of accomplishment, leading builders and homeowners to believe that they have done all that is needed, while many other important considerations have been left unaddressed. Those measures that are not properly integrated from the very beginning may actually compromise the overall performance of the home.

While energy consumption is only one aspect of a green home, it is a major concern that must be addressed throughout the design and construction of every project. The Sustainable Buildings Industry Council encourages builders to use local building materials, rely on core principles of low-energy, climate-responsive design, and use renewable (solar) energy whenever possible. However, energy use must be thought of in broader terms than simply better insulation and equipment. For example, embodied energy (the amount of energy used to produce, deliver and dispose of a product), and energy use during construction (including all those trips back and forth to the building supply store) should also be taken into consideration.

An important part, up to 25% of a home's energy consumption, is from appliances (notably the refrigerator, clothes dryer, and dishwasher), lighting loads, and plug loads, from TVs, computers, floor and table lamps, and minor appliances. Many of these appliance and plug loads depend upon choices made by your buyer, so educating them about ENERGY STAR® options is critical (see Chapter 8, Operations and Maintenance).

Knowing your energy sources and having your home rated by a certified home energy rating systems (HERS) provider ensures that you have achieved your energy goals and makes the home more market-able. Rely on the targets found in the EPA/DOE ENERGY STAR® Homes program.

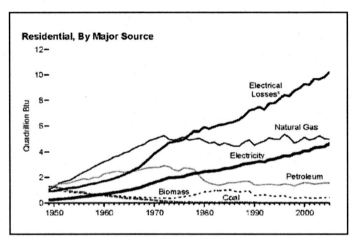

Source: Energy Information Administration/Annual Energy Review 2005.

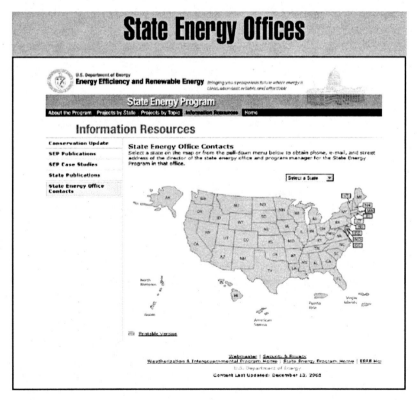

Contact and program information for State Energy Offices is best obtained from the U.S. Department of Energy's Energy Efficiency and Renewable Energy Web site: www.eere.energy.gov/state_energy_program/

Case Study: The 2030 °Challenge

With the debate on climate change hotter than ever, New Mexico architect, researcher and author, Ed Mazria has pointed a finger at one of the major culprits… the building industry… and has launched the 2030 °Challenge as the solution. It calls for a 50 percent reduction of fossil fuel used to construct and operate buildings by the year 2010, with the target of carbon neutrality by 2030. In 2006 the American Institute of Architects, the American Society of Heating, Refrigerating and Air-Conditioning Engineers, the U.S. Green Building Council, and the U.S. Conference of Mayors all adopted the 2030 °Challenge targets.

> "Rapidly accelerating climate change (global warming), which is caused by greenhouse gas (GHG) emissions, is now fueling dangerous regional and global environmental events. Data from the U.S. Energy Information Administration illustrates that buildings are responsible for almost half (48%) of all GHG emissions annually. Seventy-six percent of all electricity generated by U.S. power plants goes to supply the 'Building Sector'. Therefore, immediate action in the Building Sector is essential if we are to avoid hazardous climate change."

Source: www.architecture2030.org

Slowing the growth rate of greenhouse gas emissions and then reversing it over the next ten years will require immediate action and a concerted global effort. Buildings are the major source of demand for energy and materials that produce by-product greenhouse gases. Stabilizing emissions in this sector and then reversing them to acceptable levels is key to keeping global warming to approximately a degree centigrade (°C) above today's level.

The targets proposed are readily achievable and most buildings can be designed to use only a small amount of energy at little or no additional cost through proper siting, building form, glass properties and location, material selection and by incorporating natural heating, cooling, ventilation, and daylighting strategies. The additional energy a building would then need to maintain comfort and operate equipment can be supplied by renewable sources such as solar (photovoltaics, hot water heating, etc.), wind, and biomass.

Edward Mazria AIA, is a senior principal at Mazria Inc. Odems Dzurec an architecture and planning firm in Santa Fe, New Mexico. He is the founder of Architecture 2030. He authored the groundbreaking *Passive Solar Energy Book*, and serves as a senior analyst for the Southwest Climate Council and adjunct professor at the University of New Mexico. He speaks nationally and internationally on the subject of climate change and architecture.

Beyond Green™

SBIC believes that it is not sufficient to create a home that is simply green! Beyond Green™, the new tagline adopted by SBIC in 2006 helps convey the Council's commitment to designing and building high performance homes.

Understanding and applying a whole building approach from design to turnover makes good sense. Unlike the more traditional approach in which design decisions are made one after the other, the whole building approach relies on careful consideration and integration of other key design objectives, including: aesthetics, accessibility, cost, functionality, the safety, security, health and well-being of the occupants, along with the environmental performance of the home. This approach works equally well when applied to a single home or larger and more complex, mixed-use developments.

Although it may not be obvious at first glance, green strategies such as conserving energy and water, selecting just the right materials, focusing on durability, or ensuring great acoustical comfort, all affect which other attributes are incorporated and how successful they will be.

Some groups who previously concentrated on just one of these attributes have added green elements to their programs. Here are some examples.

Green and Affordable

Some advocates for affordable housing have decided to go green. Homes that save energy free up money for other living expenses. Santa Monica, California, for example, now has a Green Affordable Housing Checklist. Wisconsin has a Green Affordable Housing Guide in place.

The Georgia Habitat for Humanity, whose primary goal was affordability, has now recognized the importance of taking an even broader view for creating a good home and considering green features.

Green and Safe

The Institute for Business & Home Safety's "Fortified...for safer living®" program recognizes the importance of integrated design and focuses on the connection between quality construction, safety and durability.

To go Beyond Green™ homebuilders will have to consider using a more intentional *integrated* approach to design and a stronger *integrated* team process. The eight design objectives which are all, to some greater or lesser degree, important to any project are briefly described on the following pages. The final decision on which ones are primary and to what degree they are incorporated belongs to each individual builder/developer.

Green and Aesthetic

Visionary designer Sarah Susanka, (known for her beautiful residential designs and the concept of Not So Big™) incorporated green design into her 2005 Not So Big Showhouse in Orlando, Florida. SBIC, along with the U.S. DOE and the NAHB were key sponsors of this demo home.

This year the American Institute of Architects has titled its 2007 annual conference and expo "growing beyond green."

The Eight Whole Building Approach Design Objectives

Builders interested in using the whole building approach to designing their homes will consider the following eight design objectives in order to create a high performance home: accessible, aesthetic, cost effective, functional, healthy, historic, safe/secure, and sustainable.

Accessible

Pertains to the elements of the home such as heights and clearances implemented to address the specific needs of disabled people.

This design objective considers accommodating persons who are permanently disabled or temporarily disabled due to an injury. The concepts of visitability and aging in place are becoming more popular as the percentage of our aging population grows. The goal is to ensure equal use of the home for all.

Aesthetic

Pertains to the physical appearance and image of the home, its shape and spaces.

What qualifies as beautiful is open to personal interpretation and varies with client, climate, context, construction and culture. Aesthetics applies not just to the outside architecture, but to the interior design, the surrounding landscape, the neighboring buildings, and the community at large.

Cost Effective

Pertains to selecting building elements on the basis of life-cycle costs (weighing options from the conceptual stage through design development, and value engineering challenges) as well as basic cost estimating and budget control.

There is no one specific measure for true cost effectiveness, but some considerations are noted here. Does the homeowner want the lowest first cost or the lowest O&M costs? Is it the home with the longest life span? Will the house be used for a combination of purposes, such as a home office? If so, it must accommodate the public.

Functional

Pertains to spatial needs and requirements, system performance, durability, and efficient O&M.

Understanding how the home will fit its owners means defining the size and proximity of the different spaces needed for activities and equipment. Consider the owners' future needs, such as potential spatial changes from remodeling, and provide proper clearances for replacing or expanding building systems and equipment. Anticipate changing information technology (IT) and other building systems equipment.

Healthy

Pertains to the home owners' well-being and physical and psychological comfort. Air distribution, acoustics, and lighting must be controlled in all spaces throughout the home.

The indoor environment of the home can have a strong effect on homeowners' health. Excessive noise, glare, drafts, heat, humidity or cold can be potentially damaging or dangerous. Builders must design the building enclosure, building systems, equipment and appliances to work together as a unified system to achieve a truely healthy home.

Historic

Pertains to building new homes within an historic district or affecting an historic home using one of the four approaches: preservation, rehabilitation, restoration, or reconstruction.

Some practical and/or intangible benefits of historic preservation include: retaining history and authenticity; commemorating the past; increasing commercial value when homes feature materials and ornaments that are not affordable or readily available any longer.

Safe and Secure

Pertains to the physical protection of homeowners and their property from man-made and/or natural hazards.

Designing and constructing safe, secure homes and communities is a primary goal. Builders must consider different issues, such as improved indoor air quality, electrical safety, ergonomics, and accident prevention. Resisting natural hazards requires protection from hurricanes, wildfires, floods, earthquakes, tornados, and blizzards. Gated and/or guarded communities are becoming more and more popular and may often require special maintenance and equipment.

Sustainable

Pertains to the environmental performance of the home.

For an expanded definition of sustainability, see the Principles of Green Design, above.

Chapter 1   Community and Site Planning

LAND DEVELOPMENT

Smart Growth

Community growth and development can be controversial. Issues of traffic, schools, open space, and environmental protection are just a handful of the Smart Growth concerns that home builders and local governments are grappling with.

Many local home builder associations have found that a green building program changes the tenor of relations and improves opportunities for substantive dialogue on Smart Growth issues.

The reason is simple. Green building programs demonstrate that the local home builders can do more than debate an issue. They can provide concrete solutions to environmental concerns related to residential development and growth. For many builders, the good relations brought about by local government acceptance of the associations' voluntary green building programs has served as a catalyst for a more trusting and less adversarial business relationship on other issues.

Principles of Smart Growth

Increased density is the most important way to cut the use of resources in developing land. Not only does it reduce the need for certain types of infrastructure and its long-term maintenance, it also reduces the energy consumption of the home by decreasing the exposed surface area in the homes (particularly for town houses, apartments, and mixed-use structures). Properly planned higher-density development, such as the increasingly popular Traditional Neighborhood Development projects, are designed and built for easy access to schools, work, shopping, and public transportation. This type of development reduces automobile use.

Street orientation should be controlled to provide properly oriented buildings whenever allowed by density and view considerations. On east–west streets, homes can be closely spaced, with their major openings facing front and back (north and south). On north–south streets, lots should be shallower and wider, with homes set to the north side of the lot, again with major openings to the north and south. This strategy is unusual, as builders may forget that homes do not have to "face" the street to be welcoming.

Protection and enhancement of natural systems can play a key role in maintaining and enhancing our natural environment. One way builders can help is by configuring development or selecting sites that connect open spaces in ways that preserve or create wildlife corridors of forested, wetland, prairie, or other undeveloped lands. This is far more effective than creating isolated "wildlife islands." Builders can turn these lands into a home buyer asset by creating or planning for walking trails or educational signs and kiosks. Local nature-oriented nonprofits are excellent partners for such efforts. Small parcels of disconnected land or water provide little sustaining habitat for area birds, mammals, and other wildlife and vegetation.

Consider clustering homes and other buildings in a manner that preserves undeveloped lands for use as parks, with or without trails. Builders can also develop sites that promote biodiversity by landscaping using meadows, ponds, trees, and other features while minimizing lawn areas. Implementing these natural environment strategies will add value to nearby homes and ease stormwater runoff.

Access to public transportation is especially important in a previously undeveloped area. Because rapid transit is generally not available in outlying areas, building in areas with high-speed bus service linked to rapid transit or other centers is possible. Developments should also be designed to encourage walking, bicycling, and carpooling as a means of reducing conventional individual auto use.

What is a Traditional Neighborhood Development (TND)?

Traditional Neighborhood Developments, sometimes also known as neotraditional communities, seek to rediscover the principles of small towns built before World War II. Some common features of TNDs are the following:

- an interconnected network of streets to give motorists alternate routes and avoid concentrating traffic onto a single busy road;
- a town center with a small grocery store or convenience store and other essentials (including, ideally, mass transit links);
- formal plazas and greens, the most prominent of which are usually located in the center of the community;
- a mix of uses and housing types in close proximity, usually including detached houses, row houses and apartments and in the town center, apartments built above the stores;
- higher density; and
- pedestrian-oriented design, achieved through the combination of narrow street widths, sidewalks, street trees, houses which are close together—and close to the street—and alleys, which relocate the garages to the rear of the lot and remove the clutter of garage doors and driveways from the streetscape.

Source: www.newtownlaw.com/faq.htm.

Incentives for Developers and Builders

Community leaders may want to consider some or all of the following incentives:

- Waiver/reduction/deferral of fees
- Tax Incentive Programs (TIP)
- Density bonuses
- Reduced setbacks
- Reduced parking requirements
- Decreased road widths
- Flexibility in site development standards
- Flexibility in zoning code requirements
- Fast track permitting approvals
- Relaxed development requirements
- Reduced minimum lot size
- Reduced minimum setbacks
- Increased lot coverage
- Increased building height
- Reduced street standards
- Residential development in commercial zones
- Floor Area Bonus

Brownfield Sites

Brownfields are previously developed areas that may or may not have some contamination present that needs to be cleaned up before the site can be used again. Not all brownfields are created equal; some need little or no clean-up, while others may need extensive work. Builders should consider the benefits (typically prime locations and government subsidies) and balance these against the clean-up costs and disadvantages of a site. Examples of successful brownfield residential redevelopment are readily available.

Greyfield Sites

Greyfield sites are those that have been previously developed but are not contaminated. Typical examples are demolished schools, amusement parks, old malls, and at the largest scale, airports (although these invariably contain pockets of brownfield sites). These sites offer the possibility of providing a carefully planned mixed-use development within or close to existing development, filling in a "missing tooth" in the urban fabric and avoiding the development of outlying farmland. In large projects, there are often excellent opportunities for developing sizable wildlife core refuges and linking corridors. A good example of such a development is the abandoned Stapleton Airport in Denver, Colorado.

Scattered-Lot Infill Sites

One way to raise settlement density and avoid the development of open space or farmland is to "fill in" vacant lots. Infill sites are typically more expensive to develop than greyfield sites because they are scattered, access is sometimes constrained, and permits must be obtained one-by-one. The resultant added costs are partly balanced by savings from using existing infrastructure and from local incentives (mentioned previously). Local small builders can typically build on scattered-lot infill sites more economically than larger companies, because they can shepherd permits through the official channels and pay attention to the complexities of building nonrepetitive homes in tight quarters.

Open Space and Building Clustering

Clustering homes enables parks and other open spaces to be preserved for recreational or environmental purposes. Developers have found that they can cluster well-designed homes into a more densely populated community and preserve open space at a greater profit than if they had developed the area in a more traditional manner. Most home buyers are attracted to, and some willing to pay a premium for, homes that are adjacent to open spaces, recreational areas, or other amenities. Clustering can also foster an increased sense of community.

Greenfield Sites

Builders should try whenever possible to build on previously developed land in order to take advantage of existing infrastructure and to preserve existing open space, farms, forests, and recreation areas. Nevertheless, "greenfield sites," or those not previously used for buildings, remain the norm, because they are easier and faster to develop. The principles of sustainable land development mentioned above can help make these projects live up to their name and become truly green.

Paved Areas

Generally, builders should try to reduce paved areas for streets, alleys, sidewalks, and parking lots. It is possible to reduce the paved area in a subdivision by as much as 50% (15% of the land being developed rather than the more typical 22-27%). Where paved areas *are* created, consider using pervious materials to reduce stormwater runoff or using lighter colored paving materials to reduce the "heat island effect." In addition, take advantage of recycled materials, such as less expensive aggregates that reuse asphalt and concrete. Planting trees in the parking strips may help reduce the heat island effect.

During the development phase, consider narrower streets to reduce paving materials. However, the reduction in paved area can often only be achieved by adopting incentives that allow reduced road widths and parking requirements. A side benefit is that motorists slow down, allowing pedestrians and children to more safely use sidewalks, lawns, and, in smaller communities, even the street as impromptu community gathering areas.

As always, design decisions require integrated thinking. Here's a simple but interesting example. Most sidewalks are 48 to 54 inches wide, just wide enough to accommodate two people walking past one another. However, designing sidewalks to be up to 72 inches wide could help meet other goals, such as to help accommodate people with disabilities or to encourage children to play on the sidewalk rather than in the street. In any case, consider placing a sidewalk on only one side of the street.

Stormwater Management

Stormwater is defined as precipitation that does not soak into the ground or evaporate, but flows along the surface of the ground as run-off. The management of stormwater involves a combination of strategies to reduce both the run-off and the amount of pollutants that enter the run-off. Federal and state regulations require most construction sites to manage any stormwater leaving the site. Typically the site operator will be required to obtain a permit to discharge stormwater from the site. Check with the U.S. EPA or your state environmental agency. A stormwater analysis will include soil analysis, topography mapping, peak flow calculations, and run-off characteristics. It will also help measure pollutants such as fertilizers and other lawn treatments, as well as vehicular pollutants.

Important aspects of managing stormwater run-off include:

- Minimize land disturbances on the site.
- Preserve existing topography, vegetation, and landforms as much as possible.
- Separate impervious surfaces with turf, vegetation, or gravel to increase filtration and reduce run-off.
- Use pervious paving materials and avoid curbs where possible.
- Use grass paving systems as an alternative for driveways, streets, and alleys.
- Minimize the amount of road salt, animal waste, and vehicle fluids.
- Avoid using pesticides and fertilizers on landscaping.
- Switch from channeling and paved drainageways to systems that encourage sheet flow, thus reducing the need for expensive stormwater piping.
- Use open grass swales, pervious paving materials, and natural vegetation to reduce the total hard paved areas in a development.
- Ensure compliance with local and state drainage master plans and sediment control requirements.
- Make sure to remove or isolate any hazardous material on the site to prevent it getting into the stormwater run-off.

Case Study: Bigelow Homes, Chicago, Illinois

Bigelow Homes outside Chicago, Illinois has successfully created cost-effective, environmentally sustainable, community-oriented developments full of entry-level homes. One of the developments is called Home Town. Home Town uses a number of strategies to achieve its community and energy results. The following is a list of strategies used and their results:

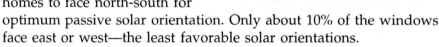
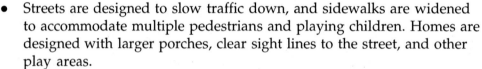

- 1,100 homes on 150 acres tripled Chicago's average density for single family development, allowing for the preservation of approximately 300 acres as woodlands and farmland.
- Roads and homes are oriented on an east-west axis, enabling homes to face north-south for optimum passive solar orientation. Only about 10% of the windows face east or west—the least favorable solar orientations.
- Streets are designed to slow traffic down, and sidewalks are widened to accommodate multiple pedestrians and playing children. Homes are designed with larger porches, clear sight lines to the street, and other play areas.
- The more efficient planning of streets and utilities allows Home Town's infrastructure to use only 33% to 50% of the embodied energy of comparable neighborhoods.
- Home Town is designed to encourage pedestrian and bicycle activity by providing ready access to commercial, retail, employment, child care, and recreation activities all within easy walking or biking distance.
- Public transportation is available within the neighborhood and links directly with mass transit and commercial areas.
- Native grasses and landscape materials are used as much as possible to minimize landscaping care.
- All construction waste was recycled.
- Each home comes with a three year, $300-per-year heating cost guarantee (twice the projected annual heating costs).
- Furnaces and hot water heaters are installed outside the air envelope of the house but inside the insulation envelope, promoting both energy-efficient operation and better IEQ.
- Fluorescent lighting is used for both interior and exterior illumination.

Source: Bigelow Homes, www.bigelowhomes.com

Land Development — Rules of Thumb

- 👍 Contact existing green building programs for resources or information on green building, even if the program does not serve your immediate area.
- 👍 Lay out streets and lots to maximize desirable orientation for homes in the development.
- 👍 Cluster homes in lower-density developments to protect and enhance open or wild areas for environmental or recreational purposes.
- 👍 Reduce paved areas as much as possible, preferably to a limit of 15% instead of the usual 22-27% of land area.
- 👍 Carefully analyze and plan for stormwater drainage and disposal on the site.
- 👍 Increase housing density whenever possible.
- 👍 Include access to public transportation when developing new sites.
- 👍 Consider the advantages and disadvantages of brownfield, greyfield, and infill sites.
- 👍 Link natural areas together to create wildlife corridors.

Additional Resources

Green Development, Rocky Mountain Institute, John Wiley and Sons, Inc. 1998.

Lessons from the Field, Northeast Midwest Institute. Offers 20 brownfield development case studies.

Site Planning and Community Design for Great Neighborhoods, Frederick D. Jarvis, Home Builder Press, National Association of Home Builders, Washington, D.C.

Conservation Design for Subdivisions, Randall G. Arendt, Island Press, Washington, D.C. 1996.

Building Greener Building Better, The National Association of Home Builders and the NAHB Research Center, Washington, D.C. 2002.

Pervious Concrete Pavements, Paul D. Tennis, Michael L. Leming, and David J. Akers, Portland Cement Association, Item Code BB302, 2004.

Web Resources

www.epa.gov/greenkit

www.arborday.org/programs/buildingwithtrees
   The Building *With* Trees recognition program is presented by the National Arbor Day Foundation in cooperation with NAHB. The program outlines tree protection practices and provides builders with opportunities to receive recognition.

www.uli.org
   Urban Land Institute

www.plannersweb.com/
   Planning Commissioners Journal

www.smartgrowth.org
   Smart Growth Network

www.nemw.org/
    Northeast Midwest Institute
www.eere.energy.gov/buildings/info/design/wholebuilding
    U.S. Department of Energy Building Technologies Program on using the
    whole building design approach.
www.savingsbydesign.com/building.htm
    Savings By Design: Whole Building Approach
www.pervious.info
    Southeast Cement Association
www.perviouspavement.org
    National Concrete Ready Mixed Association
www.cement.org
    Portland Cement Association

Interactions

See the following sections for information on how Land Development
interacts with other topics:

SITE PLANNING

Green Site Planning in Higher Density Developments

No matter what the density of a development, the site a home occupies determines major aspects of the home's design. For example, in a typical subdivision on relatively flat land, homes are almost always designed with most windows facing the street and the rear yard, with only secondary bedroom, bath, or kitchen windows facing the narrow side yards. Homes are typically designed in specific widths so they will fit on specific sizes of lot with the required setbacks.

As the density increases, the lot and street layouts determine the size and orientation of the homes more and more, until in row housing, narrow plans are developed that only have windows at the front and rear. In these cases, the site planning (except for detailed landscape design) and the amount of solar access is determined entirely during the land development stage. In a typical site plan, the builder should take advantage of the solar opportunities made available during land development, compensating in the detailed design of the home for less than ideal circumstances.

What can a builder do when setting homes in a medium- to high-density subdivision in which solar access and views have been ignored in laying out the lots and streets? Suppose, for example, that the street side of a relatively wide lot happens to be on the west. The simplest measure is to develop home plans with enough flexibility in the design so that some of the windows can be placed on the south side instead of the front or rear and so that living spaces and bedrooms, instead of closets and bathrooms, end up on the south. This may require flipping the plan right to left, or in a two-story home, flipping one story relative to the other (if that is possible). Home styles that feature informal, asymmetrical elements are easier to work with than classical "colonial" homes that emphasize symmetry at the expense of flexibility in plan layout and window placement.

Another approach that works on relatively wide lots is to orient the home sideways on a west- or east-facing lot so that its major facade faces south instead of west (toward the street). In most cases, turning the house requires some ingenious landscaping (fences, hedges, pergolas, etc.) to guide the visitor to the front door. What seems to be a problem can often turn into an opportunity for inventive design, and the end result may prove more interesting than a conventional, street-facing design.

Green Site Planning in Lower Density Developments

As density goes down and building sites become larger, there are more options for locating and designing a house to take full advantage of desirable sun, views, and breezes. Homes can more easily be protected from undesirable sun, views, wind, noise, and rain and snow. Along with freedom comes responsibility, and large sites raise new issues that must be considered during site planning. A large rural site, for example, is not likely to be served by urban utilities, and may need a septic system, a water well, and a long, paved entrance driveway. On the other hand, on a remote site, an array of photovoltaic solar cells may be selected instead of a diesel generator as a source of electricity, with the advantages of being quiet and not relying on any fossil fuel.

Of the wide variety and extent of issues that must be considered to build green on a generous site, some of the most important are the following:

- How the sun moves across the sky at the latitude of the site
- Shading by mountains, slopes, or large trees
- Shading by regular morning or afternoon fog
- Direction of prevailing snowfall and drifting (for example, entries facing northeast in New England can become completely plugged with snow, so New England Colonial farmhouses nearly always had the front door facing south or southeast)
- Direction of cold winds in winter (so protected outdoor spaces can be located out of the wind)
- Direction of cooling breezes in summer (so the home can be cooled by natural convection without mechanical air conditioning)
- Surface water drainage
- Underground water drainage and soil type
- Existing wetlands
- Attractive car access without excessive grades (especially in areas requiring salt or heating), without disrupting drainage on the site, and with areas to pile plowed snow without damaging native plants or trapping runoff water
- Attractive car parking that doesn't dominate the site and create large paved areas
- Location uphill from the septic field to avoid the need for pumping sewage
- Orientation toward desirable views and away from undesirable present or future development on adjacent sites
- Understanding of soil types and the type of plants best suited to each
- Preservation of desirable plant material, especially true native plants, and thinning or removal of undesirable plants (it pays to have a landscape architect decide which is which)
- Providing reasonable and attractive ramps or slopes up to the home's entrances, for accessibility.

Site Planning for Solar Access

Site planning should take solar access into consideration. Over the years, developers and builders have come up with flexible ways to guarantee that homes have access to the sun for the life of the building. Of course, it is not possible to always provide optimum solar access, so it is important to carefully assess shading patterns to make the best compromise. Subdivisions that have streets running within 30 degrees of east–west will have lots that face or back up to south, which is best for sun control. Subdivisions that have existing north–south streets can consider adding east–west cul-de-sacs.

In northern climates, taking full advantage of solar energy in the design of a home tends to stretch out the house's form in the east-west direction so that most living spaces can be on the south, with service spaces such as bathrooms, garage, storage, and corridors on the north, and with few east and west windows. In southern climates, the same approach to home design applies, because it is easier to control sunlight on a south-facing facade than on one facing east or west. But additional attention must be given to the use of overhangs and landscaping for shading during the cooling season.

Reduce Site Disturbance

When grading, plan activities so that heavy equipment compacts a limited area of soil and stays as much as possible where paving will occur. Prior to construction, develop a site access plan to minimize damage to the site. Indicate areas for scrap/reusable, recyclable, and waste materials, areas for staging and storing building materials, and areas where soil compaction is prohibited. During the construction phase, preserve vegetation by storing materials and performing work outside the drip line of existing trees. Transplant valuable vegetation that must be moved. Stabilize soil during and after construction by using filtration barriers, soil erosion fences, and wood chip mats at entrances. Before beginning construction, save topsoil for reuse and replace the topsoil at the end of the construction phase.

During construction, avoid creating erosion by minimizing the steepness of temporary slopes, by planning ahead for temporary site drainage, and by placing runoff barriers and sediment collectors. Silt fences or other suitable methods should be used. Incorporate language into subcontracts to ensure that other trades respect these same rules.

Illustration: Bruce Hendler

Tree Protection During Construction
To help ensure that trees are not lost during construction, consider the following:
1. During construction, the largest single killer of tree roots, and thus of trees, is soil compaction by heavy machinery.
2. The roots of most species of large, woody trees grow primarily horizontally.
3. These roots are predominantly located in the top 12" (30 cm) of soil and do not normally extend to depths greater than 3' to 7' (1 to 2 meters) yet extend outward to an average diameter of 1 to 2 times the height of the tree. As such, tree guards should be erected to protect trees during construction, but since it would be impractical in most cases to establish a complete protection zone, tree guards ❶ should reach at least to the "drip line" ❷ of the tree's crown. This action will minimize root death and the corresponding dieback of the tree's crown.

Landscaping

Careful landscaping can be aesthetically pleasing and may even save the homeowner up to 25% of the home's annual heating and cooling costs (an average of $100 to $250). Design, species selection, and placement of trees and shrubs are the keys to a beautiful, energy-efficient, water-efficient landscape, or xeriscape. Xeriscaping is a landscaping strategy that uses indigenous vegetation that is drought resistant, and once established, is able to survive largely on rainfall and available groundwater.

Consider the following energy advantages when planning a home's landscaping. An example of what an energy-efficient landscape plan can look like is shown below.

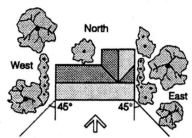

Landscaping for Summer Shade
Trees and other landscaping features may be effectively used to shade east and west windows from summer solar gains.

Landscaping Guidelines for Temperate Climates

1. Major glass areas are oriented within 20 degrees of due south and have properly sized overhangs for shading.
2. Ground cover reduces reflected sunlight.
3. Deciduous trees shade east, west, southeast, and southwest sides in summer.
4. Trellis with deciduous vine shades east wall.
5. Garage on west blocks summer sun and winter winds.
6. Windbreak of evergreen trees and shrubs to the north buffers winter winds.

Note: These strategies vary based on the local climate you are building in.

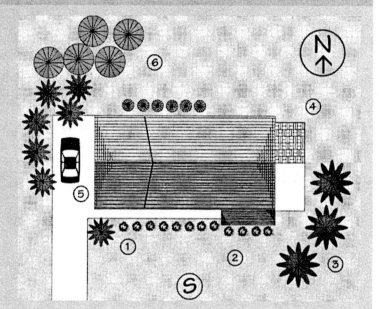

Site Planning – Rules of Thumb

👍 Lower density developments require careful design decisions in order to take full advantage of the green possibilities available on larger sites.

👍 Provide solar access to as many homes as possible during the planning process.

👍 Provide a solar orientation for homes on developed lots whenever possible.

👍 Minimize compacting of soil during construction by keeping equipment on areas that will be paved and by stockpiling topsoil.

👍 Well-designed landscaping can lower a home's heating and cooling load costs by as much as 25% through proper placement and species selection.

Additional Resources

Landscape Ecology Principles in Landscape Architecture and Land-Use Planning, Wenche E. Dramstad, James D. Olson, Richard T. Forman, Island Press. 1996.

Building Greener Building Better, The National Association of Home Builders and the NAHB Research Center, Washington, D.C. 2002.

Design With Nature, Ian L. McHarg, John Wiley and Sons, Inc. 1995.

Web Resources

www.epa.gov/greenacres/
    U.S. Environmental Protection Agency: Green Landscaping with Native Plants

www.nps.gov/dsc/dsgncnstr/gpsd/ch5.html
    National Park Service: Sustainable Site Design Philosophy

Interactions

See the following sections for information on how Site Planning affects other building considerations:

CONSTRUCTION WASTE MANAGEMENT

Why Bother?

The average home generates 3 to 5 pounds of construction waste per square foot, costing builders anywhere from $250 to well over $1,000 in disposal costs. Reducing waste lowers disposal costs. Waste reduction is realized through design and planning. Any money saved by developing and executing a waste management plan can be added directly to a builder's bottom line. By weight or volume, 60% to 80% of a builder's jobsite waste stream may be recyclable (wood, drywall, and cardboard). Metals are generated in much smaller quantities but have good recycling values. Waste placed on the jobsite by someone other than the contractor or subcontractor ("drive-by contamination") can be a factor. The key point to remember is, if you don't generate waste, you don't have to deal with it!

Developing a Waste Management Plan

Effective waste management begins with a company waste management policy and waste management plan. The policy should be a general document that acknowledges waste management as an issue and sets forth the company's general approach to waste reduction, reuse, and recycling. The waste management plan can be tailored to meet the conditions the builder faces in the community, or even on a specific site. It should address the design of homes, material purchasing practices, disposal and recycling costs, availability of outlets, and feasibility of changing worker habits. The plan should be posted on the jobsite, in the office, and given to suppliers and subcontractors. Suppliers, workers, and subcontractors should be informed of its importance. The three basic steps to developing a waste management plan are:

- Identify components of the waste stream and learn conventional disposal costs.
- Understand conditions affecting waste management decisions.
- Establish a plan that follows the waste management hierarchy of *R*educe, *R*euse, and *R*ecycle. See "Strategies to Minimize Waste Generation" later in this chapter for specific suggestions.

Waste Management Hierarchy

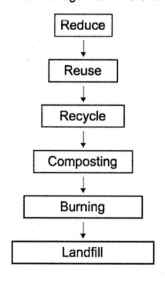

On-site waste reduction is a three-step process: reducing the amount of materials purchased and subsequently wasted, reusing as much construction waste as possible, and recycling whatever waste remains. Reducing construction waste begins with minimizing the amount of scrap and packaging materials. Recycling and waste disposal costs vary greatly from region to region and from month to month. Builders should note that developing new approaches to waste management can become profitable in the long term due to changing waste disposal fee structures, even if immediate conditions may not be favorable. Builders will need to evaluate all the conditions affecting their waste management in order to develop the most advantageous plan.

Hazardous Waste Disposal

There are two approaches to active construction hazardous waste management:

1. *Use or switch to nonhazardous substitutes.* An example is water-based paints, which have seen dramatic improvements in performance and price. Using these paints eliminates solvents and clean-up materials that can be considered hazardous. Make sure your painting subcontractor has a waste management plan.

2. *Recycle or dispose of hazardous waste at permitted facilities.* Given the complexity of federal, state, and local statutes, it can be difficult for builders to shift potential liability for hazardous waste materials generated on their jobsites. The largest sources of residential construction materials that could be considered hazardous are waste solvents, paints and coatings, and adhesives. Given the contractor's exposure under federal law, it is prudent to require subcontractor documentation of disposal methods for hazardous wastes or to directly oversee the disposal yourself.

Case Study: Construction Waste Management

Builder:	Bosgraaf Builders
Location:	Holland, MI
House types:	Approximately 55 single-family, detached homes and duplex condominium starts per year.

Approach:
Requires subcontractors to haul their own waste—no dumpsters used on site. Containers for cardboard and general waste provided behind the general contractor's office parking lot. Wood scrap hauled to office parking lot and offered to general public as "free wood." Bosgraaf has also advertised the wood scrap in a local paper and delivered to area residents.

Savings:
Disposal costs totaled approximately $80 per start; the regional average during a 1995–96 pilot program was over $400 per start.

Source: NAHB Research Center's *Residential Construction Waste Management – A Builder's Field Guide.*

Strategies to Minimize Waste Generation

The biggest opportunities for builders to reduce waste are through designing homes efficiently, optimizing purchasing, and minimizing packaging materials. These can be incorporated into contract language with suppliers and subcontractors. On-site, efficient framing techniques and reuse of materials are the best waste reduction opportunities. Wood waste is the single largest portion of the construction waste stream by both weight and volume.

Waste reduction techniques include the following:

- *Reduce packaging.* Packaging can account for up to 25% of a jobsite's waste by volume. Require suppliers to keep packaging materials or ask suppliers and product manufacturers to limit the amount of packaging. Look for materials packaged in easily reusable or recyclable materials such as cardboard.
- *Reduce waste factors* when making material take-offs.
- *Generate comprehensive, detailed construction drawings.*
- *Increase spacing of joists and studs.* This technique can reduce the amount of framing material required by 30%.
- *Create a central cutting area for wood.*
- *Separate reusable lumber,* such as 2x wood cutoffs which can be used for bridging, stakes, bracing, shims, drywall nailers, and blocking. Similarly, cutoff sheathing waste can be used for drywall stops and furring. Grind remaining wood on-site into wood chips to use as an erosion control mat at the site entrance or as mulch.
- *Use cardboard or drywall off-cuts* by grinding up for use as a soil amendment.
- *Require subcontractors to remove their own waste from the jobsite,* rather than supplying a dumpster for their use. While subcontractors may increase their contract price to include disposal, eliminating waste dumpsters from the jobsite eliminates drive-by contamination, facilitates waste separation and recycling, promotes more efficient use of materials, and improves jobsite appearance.
- *Consider precast or poured concrete or insulating concrete forms (ICF),* because they create little or no on-site waste.
- *Establish set work areas* for each trade, especially framers, to aid in separating and reusing materials.
- *Assign and empower individuals* on your staff to facilitate waste reduction and management.
- *Perform a waste audit* on each job to determine where waste can be eliminated on future jobs.
- *Site-separate waste for recycling* when sorting materials that cannot be reused. Sort into wood, cardboard, metals (wiring, steel, copper, brass, aluminum, zinc), cladding, flashing, plumbing, drywall, glass, plastics, and nonrecyclables. Plastics may have to be further separated into polystyrene, polyethylene, and PVC. Check with local recycling facilities to see what they can accept.

Strategies for Waste Recycling

There are four approaches to waste recycling:

1. *Jobsite clean-up service.* Waste management contractor establishes the service schedule and separates, transports, and tips the material. Fee structures are based on the size of the house.

2. *Jobsite commingled recovery.* Requires builders to put all waste in a conventional container and schedule service for the waste management contractor to transport and tip the materials. The materials are commingled in the container and delivered to a facility that accepts mixed waste.

3. *Jobsite separation.* Requires builders to separate the material and schedule the container service. The waste management contractor transports and tips the materials. Fees are similar to the above two approaches, but savings can be realized through separation of higher value materials.

4. *Self hauling.* Builders handle all phases of waste management: separation, containers, transport, and tipping. Disposal costs and recycling revenues are determined by vehicle cost, tipping fees, and required labor.

Construction Waste Management Procedures – Rules of Thumb

- A builder's jobsite waste is 60% to 80% recyclable.
- Create and post a waste management policy and plan.
- Consider incorporating waste management language into subcontractor agreements.
- Evaluate and update your waste management plan periodically.
- Insist that subcontractors adhere to the waste management plan.
- Properly deal with hazardous waste.
- Know local and state laws

Additional Resources

Residential Construction Waste Management: A Builder's Field Guide (NAHB-RC, January 1997) presents the cost savings and other benefits associated with waste reduction and recycling of construction waste. Case studies are presented from across the country.

Residential Construction Waste Management: A Coordinator's Guide to Conducting Workshops at the Local Level (NAHB-RC, July 1998) is a companion document to the *Builder's Field Guide*. This book systematically and comprehensively takes readers through the steps, obstacles, and opportunities in waste reduction.

On-Site Grinding of Residential Construction Debris: The Indiana Grinder Pilot (NAHB-RC) is an extensive review of a waste reduction project.

The Regulation of Solid and Hazardous Wastes: A Builder's Guide, NAHB. March 1994. 800-223-2665

Contracts and Liabilities for Builders and Remodelers, NAHB (for hazardous materials). 800-223-2665

Lund, H.F., ed., *The McGraw-Hill Recycling Handbook*, McGraw-Hill, New York. 1993.

The City of Portland, Oregon. Portland Metro, 600 NE Grand Avenue, Portland, Oregon 97232. 503-797-1650

Alameda County Waste Management Authority, 777 Davis Street, Leandro, California 94577. 510-614-1699; www.stopwaste.org

"Examples of Recent Brownfields Projects: Utilizing Solidification and Stabilization Treatment," Wilk, Charles M., Air and Waste Management Association, June 2003. Conference proceedings, Paper No. 69653.

Web Resources

http://cwm.wbdg.org
   U.S. General Services Administration: National C&D Waste Recyclers Database
www.wbdg.org/constructionwaste
   Whole Building Design Guide: Construction Waste Resource Page
www.toolbase.org/ToolbaseResources/level3
   Toolbase Services: Construction Waste Management
www.mass.gov/dep/recycle/reduce/managing.htm
   State of Massachusetts bans land-filling of most C&D waste (the nation's first statewide ban)

Interactions

See the following sections for information on how Construction Waste Management affects other building considerations:

Chapter 2   Renewable Energy

There are numerous techniques and opportunities for *conserving* energy in homes. Familiar examples, such as increased insulation levels, multiple glazings, coatings and films, controls and efficient lights and appliances are just a few. There are also a wide range of *design strategies* that rely on the forces of nature (such as the sun and natural breezes) to *provide* heating, cooling, and ventilation to the home. By controlling the sun, we can provide space heating and water heating. By controlling shade and apertures, we can provide greater thermal comfort and reduce the need for mechanical space cooling. Solar strategies can be divided into passive solar design strategies, solar water heating systems, and solar photovoltaic strategies. Reducing loads through energy conservation and providing for comfort through renewable energy work together, and should be combined in an integrated plan.

PASSIVE SOLAR DESIGN STRATEGIES

The idea of passive solar design is simple, but applying it effectively to homes does require information and attention to the details of design and construction. Some passive solar techniques are modest and low-cost and require only small changes to a builder's standard practice. At the other end of the spectrum, a complete passive design coupled with photovoltaic systems can almost eliminate a house's need for purchased energy—but at a much higher first cost.

In between are a broad range of energy-conserving passive solar design techniques. Whether or not they are cost-effective, practical, and attractive enough to offer a market advantage to any individual builder depends on specific factors such as local climate, costs, and market characteristics.

In the past, the term "passive solar design" has been misconstrued to mean just solar heating. A comprehensive list of passive solar design strategies also includes daylighting, natural ventilation, ground-coupled cooling, and peak load reduction (or shifting) with thermal mass materials such as brick, concrete, masonry, etc.

Following the Sun

One primary benefit gained from the sun is daylight. In northern latitudes and in cloudy climates, sunlight is a precious commodity to be used lavishly. However, the same northern climates where sunlight is most desired are typically also cold climates (an exception being the Pacific Northwest which, like much of Europe, has a mild climate coupled with a high latitude). In cold climates, *minimizing* glass is a high priority, in order to reduce heat loss. But *maximizing* glass is also a high priority, to compensate for cloudy days, short winter days, and low winter sun angles. Clearly, tradeoffs and compromises are called for. Maximizing glass that faces south is a good way to balance these conflicting demands. In southern latitudes, longer winter days, higher sun angles, and more intense sunlight make protection from the sun a high priority.

Ideally, sunlight should be available in the spaces where it is needed, when it is needed. For example, in a northern home, one might try to arrange rooms so that the breakfast area and possibly the owners' bedroom have an east exposure, the kitchen and family room a south exposure, with the dining area on the west. Because the sun is in the southern half of the sky for most of the year in the latitudes of the United States, maximal access to sunlight will typically lead to a design that is elongated in the east-west direction, with as many rooms as possible facing south. This is the classic passive solar home design.

Shading South-Facing Glass

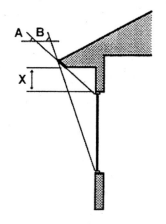

Overhang Projection Factor
The projection factor is the overhang projection divided by the distance between the bottom of the window and the bottom of the overhang.

Heat from the sun is desirable during cold weather and undesirable during warm weather. Windows facing approximately within 30 degrees of true south can be designed with overhangs to control the sun (see diagram). Typically, full sunlight is allowed in from mid-September to mid-March (autumnal equinox to vernal equinox). This approach brings in desirable solar heat during the deep winter months (as long as the glass is unshaded by trees or adjacent buildings), but it is a compromise during spring and fall. Because of the thermal lag of the earth, sunlight might be very welcome in mid-March and very unwelcome in mid-September. This is not a serious compromise, because window shades can compensate for the lack of perfection. The alternative, some kind of movable overhang, is seldom practical.

Because trees can block up to 30 - 50% of the sun, they are not desirable on the southern exposure in climates where substantial amounts of solar heating are expected and extra glass is provided for that purpose. But in climates where summer heat is a major problem, trees toward the south can make a substantial difference in the cooling load of the home, especially if they shade the roof. Unfortunately, trees close enough to the house to shade it in mid-summer may become a hazard in high winds and make it expensive or impossible to obtain wind insurance. Again, compromise is appropriate.

Shading East- and West-Facing Glass

It is important to control solar gain from the east and west to reduce air conditioning loads in all climates. The simplest way is to avoid large amounts of glass facing east or west (west solar gain is more problematic, because afternoons are on average hotter than mornings). When this is impractical, wide overhangs, such as those formed by a patio cover or trellis, can shade glass for most of the afternoon. Ordinary eave overhangs are least effective.

Another approach is to use glass that blocks solar heat. This approach, however, implies that west (and possibly east) glass should be of a different type from north and south glass. Changing glass types on different facades is almost never practical, although solar sunshades can be used with west and east glass, and omitted on the south and north. Again, a compromise is needed between providing the best views, controlling unwanted west and east solar gain, and bringing in desirable solar warmth from the south and north light from the sky.

Windows Terminology

There are three measures applied to windows that affect the control of solar energy through glass. To understand the meaning of these measures, some background is necessary.

First, we are interested in the behavior of the entire window, and not just the glass. To this end, the National Fenestration Rating Council (NFRC) has devised measures that apply to the whole window, and these are the ones you should ask for and use. Most larger window manufacturers use NFRC ratings, but smaller fabricators often do not want to spend the money for the required tests.

The Nature of Solar Radiation

Second, we need to understand something about the sun's energy. Sunlight is radiation, the same kind of radiation as radio waves and X-rays, but of a different wavelength. Sunlight also contains a small amount of ultra-violet radiation (UV)—this is what causes sunburn. About half of the remainder is visible light, while the other half is invisible infrared (IR). All this radiation, after it enters a room, is ultimately either absorbed by the materials in the room or bounced back out. All the radiation that is absorbed by the room (including light) turns into ordinary heat (long-wave IR). All of us radiate heat out to our surroundings and absorb heat from our surroundings. If something is hotter than usual, it radiates shorter IR and even visible light (as does a fire) and feels hot. If something is cold, it absorbs the heat that we emit, and this makes us feel cold on that side.

Choosing Glass in Various Climates

Suppose we can have exactly the kind of glass we want. For Example One, in a northern cold climate, we want to let in light from the sun, plus the rest of the solar heat in the IR range. So we would ask for a glass that cuts out the UV (because it is not good for fabrics and furniture) but that lets in all the visible and short-wave IR that the sun can offer. In addition, it should reflect the long-wave IR that we and our surroundings are sending out, trapping it in the room like a greenhouse.

Now let's move farther south. For Example Two, for north, east, and west elevations we want a glass that cuts out UV, lets in all the visible light, and *cuts out* the rest of the solar heat in the short-wave IR range, because it adds unwanted heat. We want to see out freely, so we don't want to cut out visible light. But we don't want any more heat than necessary, so we block the solar IR. Again, we want to reflect long-wave IR, but this time, we want to reflect back hot outside IR in summer and trap warm inside IR in winter.

Finally, we move to Miami for Example Three, where we want as little heat as possible. The only heat left that we can cut out is that produced by visible light, so we cut out as much as we can stand, taking care not to let the windows begin to look gloomy. Again, we add reflection to keep the heat outside from heating us up inside.

NFRC Definitions

We can now describe the various NFRC measures, and what they mean in practice:

- The *"solar heat gain coefficient," or SHGC*, represents the percentage of *all* the solar radiation (UV, visible light, and short-wave IR) that the whole window lets in relative to no glazing. This measure takes account of the frame, as well as the sun bouncing off the glass when it hits at a raking angle ("off-angle reflection"). The lower the SHGC, the less solar energy comes in.
- The *"visible transmittance," or VT*, represents the percentage of *visible light* that the whole window lets in, relative to a window and frame with no glazing, again taking account of off-angle reflection. The higher the VT, the clearer the window will appear.
- The *"U-factor"* is the familiar measure of transmission heat loss that we use with insulation. The lower the U-factor, the more insulating the window. One important difference between the U-factor of the glass and that of the whole window is the effect of the frame. An ordinary aluminum frame can result in a window with a U-factor of 0.60, using glass having a U-factor of 0.35. Put insulating frames around the glass, and you get a U-factor closer to that of the glass alone. So if the sticker does not show the NFRC rated U-factor, don't believe the advertised U-factor, which probably applies only to the glass.

Examples of South-Facing Glass in Various Climates

Returning to our three examples above:

- In Example One, a window for cold climates, we would like an SHGC as *high* as possible. This will certainly result in a high VT, because we will want all the visible radiation, plus the short-wave IR, to come in. We also want a low U-factor to keep the heat in.

- In Example Two, a south-facing window without shading for a mixed climate, we would like a VT as high as possible (for clear vision) coupled with an SHGC as low as possible. If you divide the VT by the SHGC, you get a measure that has no fixed name. We'll call it the "cooling coefficient." The best window of this type today will have a VT of 0.72 and an SHGC of 0.42 for a cooling coefficient of 1.7. If you are designing a passive solar home, then a south-facing window with appropriate summer shading would have both a high VT and an SHGC as high as possible. This can be accomplished with clear insulated glass (SHGC = 0.82) or with a low-e glazing with an SHGC higher than 0.6 for interior heat retention. This is as good as you can do, with more typical numbers being around 1.2 or even less. The U-factor should be low.

- In Example Three, a window for Miami, we would like as low an SHGC as possible, period. A typical window would have a VT of 0.45 or so, with an SHGC of 0.35 or less. Again, the U-factor should be low to keep out the heat.

'Tuning' Glass With Low-E Coatings

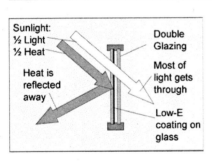

Heat, or radiation, is reflected off glass with a low-e coating.

How is all this tuning of glass possible? It is the result of some chemical magic called low-emissivity or "low-e" coatings. Depending on how many coatings there are, how they are applied, what surface of the double glazing they are applied to, and what kind of metal they are made of, manufacturers have created a bewildering array of low-e glass. They have even made single-sheet low-e glass (the coating can be difficult to clean, so check it out before specifying it). All double-glazed low-e windows tend to have a U-factor around 0.33, providing they have insulating frames.

In practice, major manufacturers tend to stock only from Example Two (south-facing window without shading) and Three glass, for the simple reason that most home construction in the United States is in the sunbelt. If you are designing a passive solar heated home for Example One and Two climate zones, you may well have to special order glass with a high VT and a high SHGC, or find a manufacturer who will fabricate a window using it.

Shading Glass With Overhangs and Landscaping

A roof overhang is a fixed building feature that, when properly sized, helps shade against unwanted solar heat gain and requires no operation by the homeowner. Like passive solar windows, roof overhangs are most effective when they are used on windows within 30 degrees of true south. For east and west windows, consider the use of vertical louvers instead of overhangs. Roof overhangs must be carefully designed to block unwanted sun (typically in summer and early fall), but not block spring, fall, or winter sun that is desirable for heating.

The optimal geometry of a roof overhang on the south side of a home depends on the home's latitude. Refer to the illustration in the "Shading South-Facing Glass" section earlier. In general, overhangs should be designed with a separation between the window head and the underside of the roof (distance X), so that the low winter sun can enter (angle A) and the high summer sun will be blocked (angle B).

Landscaping can help or hinder the energy efficiency of a home. Ideally, landscaping should be used to provide summer shading, enhance natural ventilation by cooling the microclimate around the home, allow winter solar gain and daylighting, and block prevailing winter winds. Locate deciduous trees to shade the east and west sides of the house, but only in areas that are more than 60 degrees east or west of due south from the house. In particular, west and southwest facades should be shaded from low-angle afternoon sun that causes overheating. Depending on glazing location, mixing smaller and larger trees on the east and west side of the house may also offer useful shading, but be careful not to block summer breezes. Other landscaping ideas for summer shading are:

- Vine-covered trellises or patio covers on east and west sides
- Shrubbery or other plantings to shade paved areas
- Use of ground cover to prevent glare and heat absorption
- Trees, fences, shrubbery, or other plantings to channel summer breezes
- Deciduous trees on the east and west sides of the house to balance solar gain in all seasons

Care should be exercised in placing or working with deciduous trees on the south side of a home, because even with their bare branches, these trees can block as much as 30% of the available winter solar energy. Tree placement to block cold winter winds varies with location, but typically means placing evergreen trees on the north, northeast, or northwest facades. See Chapter 1, Community and Site Planning, "Landscaping," for diagrams and more information.

How to Use Thermal Mass

Some heat storage capacity, or thermal mass, is present in the normal construction features of all houses. This is enough mass to support the small amount of south glazing used in "sun-tempered" designs. More extensive use of passive solar glazing calls for additional thermal mass and thoughtful consideration regarding the placement of the added mass. Thermal mass helps prevent high midday interior temperatures in summer or on sunny days in winter. Thermal mass can also be integrated with the mechanical heating and cooling systems to result in a more thermally comfortable house. In a passive solar house, high-performing thermal mass materials such as brick, masonry, poured concrete, precast concrete, or tile are usually placed in the floor or interior walls where sunlight will fall directly on them (this is called "direct gain" or "direct storage").

Most of the concrete and masonry materials used in passive solar design have similar capabilities to absorb heat on a pound-for-pound basis. Thus the major factor affecting performance is the density of the material; generally, the higher the density the better. To ensure cost effectiveness, try to employ thermal mass materials that serve multiple purposes within the home, such as providing structural support or dividing rooms.

Generally, thermal mass should be relatively thin (generally 2" to 4") and spread over a wide area.

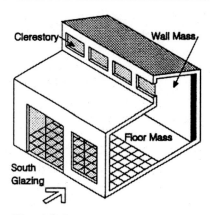

Direct Gain
Direct gain is the most common passive solar system in residential applications.

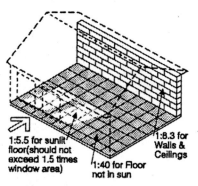

Mass Location and Effectiveness
Additional mass must be provided for south-facing glass over 7% of the floor area. The ratio of mass area to additional glass area depends on its location within the direct gain space.

Thickness of Thermal Mass

For most thermal mass materials, their energy effectiveness increases up to a thickness of about 4 inches. Mass thicker than 4 inches typically does not absorb and release heat quickly enough to be effective and worth the additional investment.

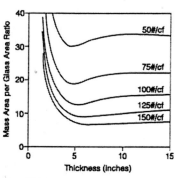

Mass Thickness
The effectiveness of thermal mass depends on the density of the material and thickness. This graph is for wall or ceiling mass in the direct-gain space. The ratio of 8.3 was used earlier as a representative value.

Ways of Providing Thermal Mass

In most cases, the easiest way to add thermal mass is to use an exposed concrete slab. It can be covered with brick (especially face brick and pavers), stone, or tile, or it can be stained or painted. It is important that it be exposed to direct sunlight and not "insulated" with rugs or carpets. Today's popular stained or stamped concrete is an ideal thermal storage medium. A good strategy is to expose a strip about 8 feet wide along the south wall next to the windows where the winter sun will fall directly upon it (assuming the glazing runs close enough to the floor that the strip near the wall is unshaded). Because of its weight, adding thermal mass into the flooring of homes with crawlspaces or basements requires heavier framing, unless the entire floor is structural concrete. Finishing the slab with a dark color gives the best energy performance. A matte finish on the floor will

reduce glare as well as reflected sunlight, thereby increasing the amount of heat captured by the mass. If the goal is to dissipate excess solar heat in a hot climate, it pays *not* to insulate under the slab, so that it acts as a heat sink. But wherever the winters are cold, the slab should be carefully and completely insulated from ground contact, so that its stored heat is not transferred into the ground under the home. The edges of the slab should also be

well insulated. When insulating the slab edge, either by insulation outside the slab or by insulation running between the foundation wall and slab edge, it is important to provide protection from termites, which can use the foam insulation as a route to the interior framing.

For northern climates, storing solar energy is most important during the winter, when sun angles are low. Assuming this low sun is not blocked by trees or adjacent buildings, it can often shine all the way across a room, directly onto a masonry wall. However, as the sun sweeps across the sky, only parts of the wall will be exposed to direct sunlight only part of the time. Therefore, it doesn't matter much whether the wall gets direct sun or not, as long as it gets sunlight that bounces around the room. Thus, a 2" to 4" layer of dense material (brick, stone or tile veneer, or concrete) used on wall surfaces in southfacing rooms can function effectively as thermal mass. Increasingly, entire homes are being built out of precast concrete. As long as there is continuous and effective thermal insulation between the outside and the interior concrete walls and floors, all this mass can help store the warmth of the sun. Similarly, the outer walls of an interior masonry fireplace can help store solar energy.

Case Study: Passive Solar Design

For only $100,000, a couple in cloudy Portland, Oregon, built a passive solar-designed home in their neighborhood's traditional architecture style. The 1,250 square foot home was built in 1994 and saves about $150 per year on heating and cooling bills. When the avoided cost of not having to buy an air conditioner is

The Cunningham/ Pinon home blends in aesthetically with the older homes in the neighborhood. The 155 square feet of south-facing windows provide direct solar gain to every room in the house.

taken into account, the home was built at a cost savings. Even without considering that avoided cost, the home was built at a 1% ($1,000) premium: $500 savings on the heating system, $700 added cost for windows, and $800 added cost for insulation.

To optimize the passive solar potential, 155 square feet of glass was placed on the south side of the home (three times the conventional amount for a home this size) under long overhangs that shade the summer sun. Windows on the north and east were minimized and west windows were shaded with elongated overhangs. The home is well sealed and uses added fiber glass batt insulation of

R-50 in the ceiling and attic and R-23 in the walls. R-15 rigid insulation can be found under the tile-covered, concrete slab floor, which holds the winter sun's heat.

When passive solar heat is not enough, the home is heated by a quiet, in-floor, hydronic radiant heating system with advanced electric wall heaters upstairs (total cost was $500 less than a furnace with a forced air system). The passive solar designed overhangs, window placement, thermal mass, and air sealing eliminated the need for mechanical cooling. Natural ventilation and ceiling fans provide what cooling is needed. Calculations show passive solar design savings of 50% for the cooling load and 16% for the heating load. An additional 26% heat savings resulted from the extra insulation and lower infiltration rate. Total results: 50% cooling load reduction, 42% heating load reduction.

Other notable green aspects of the home include natural linoleum flooring, low-VOC paints and finishes, recycled carpet, a formaldehyde-free kitchen and bathroom cabinets, and a thermosiphon solar water heater. (The solar water heater savings are not included in this case study.)

Source: U.S. DOE.

In order to reduce heat loss, north-facing windows are kept to the minimum needed for daylighting and views. West windows are shaded by the porch overhang, which cuts out unwanted summer heat and glare.

Case Study: An Affordable, Energy-Efficient Passive Solar Home

We designed and built an 1,800-sq. ft. house, plus a screened porch, for $165,000, well below local costs for conventional custom homes in our area. Wherever possible, the house is constructed of environmentally sensitive materials, meaning they are nonpolluting or low in toxicity and may be recycled. Inexpensive to light, heat and cool, the house should last for well over 100 years with only minimal maintenance. The [homeowners] got what they really wanted: a "green" house they could afford.

—James Cameron and Kathleen Jardine, "Building for Affordability and Energy Efficiency," *Fine Homebuilding* magazine, Houses 1999
www.taunton.com/finehomebuilding/pages/h00002.asp

Passive Solar Design -- Rules of Thumb

- 👍 The increased amount of glazing in passive solar designed homes may add value to the home. Appropriately oriented increased window area offers sunny interiors and better views, amenities home buyers are looking for. Combined with improved comfort achieved by high-performance glazing, this leads to higher owner satisfaction and better resale values.
- 👍 The use of low-emissivity (low-e) glass will improve the performance of almost any home.
- 👍 The energy effectiveness of thermal mass materials generally increases up to a thickness of about 4 inches.
- 👍 Denser thermal mass materials are more effective at storing and releasing heat.
- 👍 Thermal mass materials placed in direct sunlight perform most effectively.
- 👍 If the thermal mass is not in direct sunlight, use three to four times as much area.
- 👍 Do not cover thermal mass materials with carpet or rugs.
- 👍 Select an appropriate mass color. Dark colors absorb the most solar energy.

Additional Resources

The Passive Solar Design and Construction Handbook, Steven Winter Associates, Norwalk, CT. 1998.

Passive Solar Design Strategies: Guidelines for Home Building, Sustainable Buildings Industry Council, Washington, D.C. 1994. Detailed passive solar design information, including climate-specific worksheets and examples.

www.nfrc.org
The National Fenestration Ratings Council Web site provides an industry-standard rating for use by manufacturers. Helpful window selection information is also available.

Guide to Stained Concrete Floors, Bob Harris, Decorative Concrete Institute, PCA Item code LT283, 2004; www.cement.org.

Web Resources

www.ases.org
   American Solar Energy Society
www.seia.org
   Solar Energy Industries Association
www.eere.energy.gov/consumer/your_home/windows_doors_skylights
   U.S. Department of Energy
www.eere.energy.gov/buildings/info/homes/solarpassive.html
   U.S. Department of Energy: Passive Solar Design
www.sunplans.com/html/passive_solar
   Sun Plans, Inc.: About Passive Solar
www. concretethinker.com
   Portland Cement Association
www.concretehomes.com
   Portland Cement Association
www.efficientwindows.org/selection.cfm
   Efficient Windows Collaborative (EWC) members have made a commitment to manufacture and promote energy-efficient windows. This site provides unbiased information on the benefits of energy-efficient windows, descriptions of how they work, and recommendations for their selection and use.

Interactions

See the following sections for information on how Passive Solar Design Strategies affect other building considerations:

SOLAR WATER HEATING SYSTEMS

Water heating uses about 17% of the energy in U.S. homes and ranks as the second largest household energy expense after space conditioning. To minimize this big energy user, consider installing a solar domestic hot water (DHW) system. They work in all climates, though freeze protection and larger collectors increase the cost in colder, less sunny regions. A typical solar DHW system is sized to provide up to 70% of the annual water heating load. Most solar water heaters operate by preheating water for a standard water heater that, when needed, operates as a backup to increase the water temperature. Thus, the temperature and availability of hot water is not compromised in the process of saving energy. There are two categories of solar DHW systems: indirect and direct systems. Indirect pumped systems can be used in any climate and indirect thermosyphon and batch systems can be used in climates with occasional light freezes. Direct systems are generally only suitable for nonfreezing climates.

Systems range in cost from $1,500 to over $5,000. Solar DHW systems can be very reliable with proper installation and maintenance.

Thermosyphon Systems

A thermosyphon system heats water or an antifreeze fluid such as glycol. The fluid rises by natural convection from collectors to the storage tank, which is placed at a higher level. No pumps are required. If the system heats domestic water directly, water should not be hard or acidic, because it will cause scale deposits that will block collector fluid passages. Indirect thermosyphon systems can be used in moderately cold climates, but the connecting piping and storage tank must be protected from freezing. Direct thermosyphon systems can be used only in nonfreezing climates, or in cold climates if completely contained within the building's conditioned space.

Direct Circulation Systems

A direct circulation system pumps water from a storage tank to collectors during sunny hours. Freeze protection is obtained by recirculating hot water from the storage tank or by flushing the collectors (a process called "draindown"). Because recirculating hot water greatly increases energy use, direct circulation systems should be used only in those areas where freezing is infrequent. Note that these methods of freeze protection are less reliable than those found in other types of solar DHW systems.

Drain-Back Systems

In a drain-back system, water from a storage tank is circulated through the solar collectors and back to the tank. Heat is transferred to potable water through a heat exchanger in or near the storage tank. When no solar heat is available, the collector fluid is drained by gravity to avoid freezing.

Closed Loop Systems

A closed loop system circulates anti-freeze through a pressurized closed loop. Heat is transferred to potable water through a heat exchanger. The most commonly used fluid for freeze protection is a water–propylene glycol solution.

Batch / Integral Collector Storage Systems

A batch or integral collector storage system uses a combined solar collector and storage tank unit, which is located on the roof. When hot water is used, water main pressure drives warm water from the solar collector/tank to the auxiliary tank inside the house. This design needs no pumps or electronic controls. The heat capacity of the water in the collector is sufficient to avoid freezing during moderately cold nights, but the water in the connecting piping can freeze at temperatures around 32 degrees. A special freeze prevention drip valve should be used on a batch water heater. Depending on how they are sized, batch heaters typically store 30 to 50 gallons of hot water and can supply 15% to 40% of a family's yearly demand.

Design and Installation Recommendations

The performance of a solar water heating collector remains high across a wide range of panel tilt angles and orientations. For maximum year-round performance, the collectors should be tilted from the ground at an angle

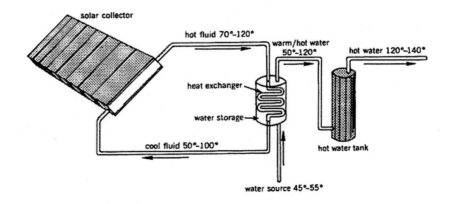

equal to or slightly less than the latitude. For example, the ideal angle for Atlanta is 35 to 45 degrees, but angles of 20 to 50 degrees are acceptable. An orientation within 45 degrees to the east or west or south is also acceptable. Therefore, collectors may be laid flat against most sloped roofs, as long as the pitch is not too steep and is within 45 degrees of due south.

The Solar Rating and Certification Corporation (SRCC) tests collectors and solar water heating systems and certifies products. Certified products can be obtained from several manufacturers listed in the SRCC Product Directory. Any system purchased should be installed by an experienced solar contractor. Some solar collectors have integral flashings that can be installed into roofing assemblies in a manner similar to skylights.

Pre-Plumbing for Solar Water Heating

Installing solar water heating pre-plumbing allows for easy future installation of an active solar system. Install pre-plumbing if the home meets the following criteria: 1) the home's roof can support solar panels within 45 degrees of due south, and 2) there is space for plumbing between the roof and the utility room or other location where you might locate a solar water storage tank.

The cost of approximately $250 will save homeowners who later install such a system a lot of time and expense. To install the pre-plumbing, run two 3/4" type M copper lines and a 24V control wire down an interior wall from the highest point of the roof that will hold the solar panels to the utility room or location of the future solar tank. Be sure to insulate the copper lines to a minimum of R-6 and to solder all joints with lead-free solder.

Solar Water Heating – Rules of Thumb

👍 Always have solar water heating systems installed by an experienced contractor.

👍 A typical solar DHW system is sized to provide 70% of the annual hot water heating load.

👍 For maximum year-round collection, the collectors should be 1) tilted from the horizontal at an angle within 20 degrees of the latitude and 2) at an orientation within 45 degrees to the east or west of true south.

👍 Collectors for any type of solar water heater should be located as close as possible to the water heater tank to minimize the amount of connecting pipe.

👍 Systems often require higher maintenance in freezing climates than they do in nonfreezing climates.

👍 In most of the continental United States where freezing is possible, indirect closed loop or drain-back systems are often most appropriate. In very warm areas where freezing will rarely or never occur, thermosyphon, batch, or other direct systems may be practical.

👍 Consider and develop strategies for the following issues in your solar

DHW design: preventing stagnation, providing freeze protection, avoiding calcification and corrosion, and leakage.

👍 Consider pre-plumbing homes to accommodate a future solar water heating system installation.

👍 Be certain that adequate hot water storage is provided for the collector area, typically 1.5 gallons for every SF of collector.

Additional Resources

Solar Energy International, P.O. Box 715, 76 S. 2nd St., Carbondale, CO 81623. 970-963-8855

Web Resources

www.ases.org
   American Solar Energy Society
www.seia.org
   Solar Energy Industries Association
www.eren.doe.gov/solarbuildings
   U.S. Department of Energy: Solar Buildings
www.solarenergy.org
   Solar Energy International
www.nesea.org/buildings/info/solarwater.html
   Northeast Sustainable Energy Association: Solar Water Heating

Interactions

See the following sections for information on how Solar Water Heating Systems affect other building considerations:

SOLAR PHOTOVOLTAIC STRATEGIES

Photovoltaic technology (often referred to as "PV") converts sunlight into electricity. PV produces electricity directly from the electrons freed by the interaction of sunlight with semiconductor materials in the PV cells. PV allows you to produce your own electricity with no noise, no air pollution, and no moving parts. A PV system will never run out of "fuel." PV is being used today in many applications. The simplest systems power many of the small calculators and wrist watches we use every day. Larger systems provide electricity for pumping water and powering communications equipment and traffic signals. Although it is not yet commonplace, PV can be used to light our homes and run our appliances.

The basic building block of PV technology is the solar "cell." PV cells are wired together to produce a PV "module," the smallest PV component sold commercially. These modules range in power output from about 10 watts to about 300 watts. A PV system tied to the utility grid consists of one or more PV modules connected to an "inverter," a device that converts the system's direct current (DC) electricity to alternating current (AC), which is compatible with the utility grid and able to power lights, appliances, computers, and televisions. Although seldom used with grid-connected systems, batteries are an essential component of remote "stand alone" systems. All the wiring and equipment other than the collectors is called the "balance of system," or BOS.

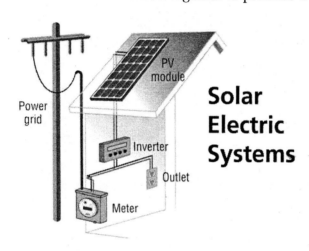

Solar Electric Systems

A PV system that is connected to the power grid is essentially a mini-utility system. When a home requires more electricity than the PV array is generating (for example, at night), the need is met by power from the utility grid. When the home requires less electricity than the PV array is generating, the excess is fed back to the utility. Used this way, the utility backs up the PV like batteries do in stand-alone systems. At the end of the month, a credit for electricity sold gets deducted from charges for electricity purchased. If the utility has a "net metering" provision, electricity is sold back at the same rate at which it is purchased. Without net metering, the cost of PV-generated power increases.

In addition to the PV modules, the homeowner must purchase balance-of-system equipment. This includes power conditioning equipment, wires, conduit, fuses, safety disconnects, outlets, and metal structures for supporting the modules. If the system is stand-alone, it will have batteries and associated equipment and may not have an inverter (special DC appliances are available).

Inverters

For normal grid-connected PV systems, the power fed back into the grid must meet the utility's standards of quality. Besides the inverter, which changes the DC power from the collectors into AC, sophisticated electronics are needed to ensure that the sold power is "clean" and in the proper phase.

Orientation

The orientation of a PV system (the compass direction that the system faces) will affect performance. In the United States, the sun is always in the southern half of the sky and is higher in the summer and lower in the winter. Usually, the best location for a PV system is a south-facing roof, but roofs that face east or west may also be acceptable.

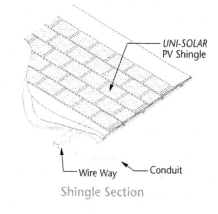

Shingle Section

Here are three factors to consider when determining whether your site is appropriate:

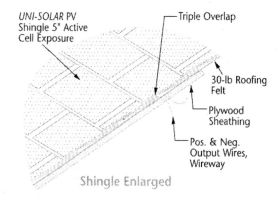

Shingle Enlarged

- For maximum daily electric energy output, PV modules should be exposed to the sun for as much of the day as possible, especially during peak sun hours of 10 a.m. to 3 p.m.

Shingle Plan

- The exposure must be free of obstructions such as trees, mountains, chimneys, other roofs, and buildings that might shade the modules. Consider both summer and winter paths of the sun, as well as the growth of trees and future construction that may cause shading.
- Climate, orientation, and altitude will affect the number of PV modules necessary to generate a given amount of electricity. Seasonal variations affect the amount of sunlight available to power a PV system.

If your location limits the physical size of the system, you may want to install a system that uses more efficient PV modules, which produce more electricity from a given area of collector. The collectors can either be mounted over a roof on metal supports, or, for some designs, can be integrated into the roofing material (i.e., shingles, tile, etc.).

Talk to an Experienced Professional

Consult an experienced PV system designer or system supplier who will have detailed technical specifications and other necessary information. Here are several suggestions for identifying help:

- Check the National Center for Photovoltaics, which is posted at the following Web address: www.nrel.gov/ncpv/ pvmenu.cgi?site+ncpv&idx=3&body=overview.html
- Contact the Solar Energy Industries Association for a list of solar service providers (202-383-2600), or visit their Web site at www.seia.org
- Contact your utility company to see which vendors it might recommend.

You will not need to know all the details of designing, purchasing, and installing the PV system when choosing a PV professional. Rely on their expertise to design and install a system that meets the needs of the buyer or homeowner.

Interconnection Agreements

Connecting your PV system to the utility grid will require you to enter into an interconnection agreement and a purchase and sale agreement. Federal law and perhaps your state's public utility commission regulations require utilities to supply you with an interconnection agreement. The interconnection agreement specifies the terms and conditions under which your system will be connected to the utility grid.

National standards for utility interconnection of PV systems are quickly being adopted by many local utilities. The most important of these standards focuses on inverters. Traditionally, inverters simply converted the DC electricity generated by PV modules into the AC electricity used in our homes. More recently, inverters have evolved into remarkably sophisticated devices to manage and condition power.

Financial Incentives

To make PV systems affordable, several states are offering financial incentives through rebates and other programs. These include:

- *Net metering.* Increasingly, state laws require utilities to offer net metering, in which the meter spins backward when the PV system feeds unused power back into the grid.
- *Property and sales tax.* Tax incentives may include exemption of sales tax on the PV system purchase, exemption of property tax, or state personal income tax credits.
- *Buydowns.* Rebates and buydowns, typically based on the power of the system, are a crucial aid in defraying the high capital cost of a PV system.

Remember, the more energy efficient your homes are, the greater the impact the PV systems will have. Measures such as increased insulation and energy-efficient lighting, appliances, and windows will of course drastically reduce your home's use of electricity. The larger the PV system is relative to the home's need for electricity, the more crucial is net metering to making the system economical.

Case Study: Energy Independence Through Photovoltaics

In 2001 the "Solar Patriot" house was constructed on the National Mall in Washington, D.C., as part of Solar FORUM 2001. During the 10 days it was open, more than 25,000 visitors—among them members of Congress, U.S. DOE officials, and the head of the EPA—toured the home to learn about its energy-efficiency and renewable-energy features. Afterwards, the Solar Patriot was transported to Purcellville, Virginia, where it became the home of Carol and Alden Hathaway and their three children. The 2,880-square foot, five-bedroom, Colonial-style, modular home was designed and built by Don Bradley, President of Solar Strategies in Philadelphia.

Photo by Don Bradley

The Solar Patriot uses a 6 kW solar photovoltaic (PV) system, which consists of thin film amorphous silicon solar modules integrated into the metal standing seam roof (4 kW) on the main house, and monocrystalline solar panels (2 kW) on the garage. Most of the home's energy needs are supplied by the PV systems. The Solar Patriot connects to the local power grid but is not dependent on it because of its prioritized loads. Since the Hathways moved into the neighborhood in August 2001, they have been selling "green" power back to their utility company. There have been numerous power outages, but they were unaffected by all of them.

Case Study: Energy Independence Through Photovoltaics (continued)

The Solar Patriot's "whole building" approach relies on passive solar strategies such as building orientation, window location and size, and window shading, which help lower the overall energy load. In addition, the home features a solar water heating system, a geothermal heat pump, added insulation, and other enhancements such as compact fluorescent lighting. As a result, the home requires only 24 kWh per day of electricity, compared with 55 kWh for a non-solar house of the same size.

The total cost for the house was 7% to 10% greater than a conventional home with similar amenities. The Hathaways figure they will break even on the higher mortgage in seven or eight years, and start saving money from that point on. The Solar Patriot and its PV system has produced more energy than the Hathaways use, making it a Zero Energy Home (ZEH). The ZEH concept provides improved comfort, reliability, security, and environmental sustainability by incorporating climate-specific design, passive solar heating and cooling, natural daylighting, energy-efficient construction, energy-efficient appliances and lighting, and solar thermal and solar electric (PV) systems.

Bradley is part of one of four teams working with DOE and its National Renewable Energy Laboratory (NREL) promoting the ZEH concept to the single-family, new-home construction industry. The ZEH initiative seeks to build homes that perform at least 50% more efficiently while meeting their own energy needs. Visit the Solar Buildings Program Web site at www.eere.energy.gov/buildings/info/homes/usingsolar for more information.

Renewable and Efficiency Features of the Solar Patriot

Heating and Cooling
- ECR Technologies Earth-link geothermal heat pump system

Fireplace
- Heat n Glow wood burning fireplace insert

Water heating
- Closed loop system consisting of two 4 x 8 Duke Solar Panels
- Hot water loop off geothermal systems as backup

Passive solar strategies
- Direct gain passive design with cement board and tile floors used as mass
- South-facing low-e windows
- 2-foot overhangs
- Cross ventilation with operable windows
- Sun Tube skylight used in second floor master bathroom for daylighting

Photovoltaics
- 4 kW UniSolar thin-film array on standing seam roof of house
- 2 kW array of BP Solar modules on garage roof
- Two Trace SW-4048 inverters
- Eight 200 amp-hour batteries backup
- Loads prioritized in case of power failure

Water conservation
- Low-flow showerheads, faucets, and toilets

Insulation
- R-45 ceiling
- R-24 exterior walls

Other
- Ceiling fans
- Compact fluorescent lights

Source: Solar Today.

Photovoltaic Strategies — Rules of Thumb

👍 Remember, the more energy efficient your homes are, the greater the impact the PV systems will have. Measures such as increased insulation and energy-efficient lighting, appliances, and windows will of course drastically reduce your home's use of electricity.

Additional Resources

Builder's Guide: Hot-Dry & Mixed-Dry Climates, U.S. Department of Energy's Building America program, Joseph Lstiburek, Ph.D. September 2000. A systems approach to designing and building homes that are healthy, comfortable, durable, energy efficient, and environmentally responsible.

Sustainable Building Technical Manual: Green Building Design, Construction, and Operations, Public Technology, Inc., U.S. Green Building Council, U.S. Department of Energy, and U.S. Environmental Protection Agency. 1996. A good section on photovoltaic design and installation. PTI, 1301 Pennsylvania Ave. NW, Washington, D.C., 20004-1793. 800-852-4934; pti.nw.dc.us

Photovoltaics in the Built Environment: A Design Guide for Architects and Engineers, National Renewable Energy Laboratory, DOE/GO publication #10097-436. September 1997.

A Builder's Guide to Energy Efficient Homes in Georgia, Georgia Environmental Facilities Authority Division of Energy Resources. September 1999. Southface Energy Institute, Inc., 241 Pine Street, Atlanta, GA 30308. 404-872-3549; www.southface.org

A Consumer's Guide to Buying a Solar Electric System. Produced for the U.S. Department of Energy by the National Renewable Energy Laboratory. www.nrel.gov/ncpv/pdfs/26591.pdf

Institute of Electric and Electronic Engineers, P929: Recommended Practice for Utility Interface of Photovoltaic Systems. Institute of Electrical and Electronic Engineers, Inc., New York, NY (1998).

Underwriters Laboratories, UL Subject 1741: Standard for Static Inverters and Charge Controllers for Use in Photovoltaic Power Systems (First Edition). Underwriters Laboratories, Inc., Northbrook, IL (December 1997).

National Center for Photovoltaics, www.nrel.gov/ncpv

Database of State Incentives for Renewable Energy (DSIRE), www.dsireusa.org/

Web Resources

www.fsec.ucf.edu
    Florida Solar Energy Center
www.nrel.gov/docs/fy04osti/34279.pdf
    U.S. Department of Energy: Heat Your Water with the Sun
www1.eere.energy.gov/solar/
    U.S. Department of Energy: Solar Buildings
www.seia.org
    Solar Energy Industries Association
www.ases.org
    American Solar Energy Society
www.solarenergy.org
    Solar Energy International

Interactions

See the following sections for information on how Solar Photovoltaic
Strategies affect other building considerations:

Chapter 3   The Building Envelope

Why the Envelope Is Important

The home's envelope (enclosure) separates the living environment from the outside environment in order to provide protection from the weather, intruders, pests, noise, and dirt, to control the entry of sunlight, and, most important, to maintain comfort. The envelope of a home includes part or all of the structure that holds up and forms the roof and that resists lateral loads from wind or earthquakes. This dual role of the envelope is a blessing, because it is economical, and a curse, because its two functions can conflict with each other. A durable and effective envelope is a key element in a green home, because all that goes on within the home depends on its proper functioning.

What Does the Envelope Include?

In this chapter and in Chapter 7, Materials, the envelope is subdivided as follows:

- Foundations
- Walls and floors
- Wall cladding/exterior surfaces
- Roofs
- Insulation and air sealing
- Windows

In a typical one-story home on a concrete slab, the envelope includes the slab, the outside walls, and the roof structure. If the wall structure is concrete or masonry, it is likely to be covered with stucco or brick on the exterior, with insulation and gypsum board on the inside.

If the wall structure is framed, the framing can be either wood or steel. Wood-framed homes located in temperate climates are insulated between the 2 x 4 (or 2 x 6 where greater insulation is required) framing members. In most steel-framed homes (and many wood-framed homes), an additional layer of insulation occurs either inside or, more commonly, outside the framing. The outside surface will be cladding (brick, stone, wood, wood composites, fiber cement, etc.) along with an air barrier and/or water resistant material such as asphalt paper or housewrap. Wood-framed homes are typically sheathed with wood structural panels (OSB or plywood) to provide resistance to wind and seismic loads. The inside surface is typically gypsum wallboard possibly with a vapor retarder installed directly to the studs.

In a typical two-story home with a basement or crawlspace, the envelope includes the foundation walls and the insulated edges of the floor structures in addition to the walls and roof. At the roof, the weather-protective roofing and the energy-protective layer of attic insulation are separate from each other. In some cases, the roof insulation occurs directly under the roof, creating a cathedral ceiling over usable space, or "cathedralized" when insulation is placed at roof level in a trussed roof.

Building Science in Transition

Building science is crucial in understanding how homes work. Long-held theories and ideas are being challenged, and accurate data is flowing in from well-instrumented test sites and from field monitoring of new and existing homes. Building scientists seldom disagree about the facts. Controversy arises over how much emphasis to give each of the many factors that influence the behavior of building elements. For example, one investigator may approve of a technique because it has beneficial consequence X, while another investigator will disapprove of the same technique because it has undesirable consequence Y. Both X and Y occur, so both investigators are correct. But which is more important, the good result X or the bad result Y? How much X and how much Y actually occur in the field?

Adding to the controversy, some building code provisions (for example, crawlspace ventilation) are based on outdated theories coupled with sparse evidence drawn from building construction technology no longer in use. Yet, because these requirements have been an important feature of the building codes used by two generations of designers, builders, and investigators, they seem sacrosanct. It should not be a surprise that dislodging old ideas in favor of newer, more solidly based findings may take several years of discussion, compromise, and education.

Foundations

Where the frostline is relatively deep, homes are typically built on crawlspaces or basements. If a basement is not needed or desired, either a slab or crawlspace is used. Crawlspaces must be designed to allow for visual inspection, so a leak (either from inside or from outside) can be readily detected. Provided it is insulated at the perimeter, a slab on grade eliminates this problem. It also has many other advantages in colder climates, including its ability to store and release solar-generated heat, and if properly insulated below, to form an ideal substrate for radiant heating.

In colder climates, most builders find it easier to build a floor over a crawlspace than to carefully backfill for a slab. The first of these problems can be resolved by erecting the bearing walls on strip foundations independent of the slab, which can then be poured after the home is closed in. The second can be overcome by using a frost-protected shallow foundation (FPSF), where a skirting of insulation is placed around the outside of the foundation, trapping ground heat and making deep frostwalls unnecessary. These foundations are described more fully in Chapter 7, Materials.

If a basement is present, heating equipment and piping or ductwork is invariably located in the basement. Heat loss from basements therefore becomes an important part of the home's energy consumption. Achieving a high rating in most Home Energy Rating programs requires that the basement be sealed and insulated and that walls be insulated whenever a basement is converted to living space. One technology that automatically insulates the basement wall very effectively is insulating concrete forms (ICF), where concrete is poured into modular forms made of foam insulation. These are more fully discussed in Chapter 7, Materials.

Moisture Control Techniques

Careful attention to water movement (foundation drainage systems, house perimeter grading, and flashing details) and vapor movement (air sealing details and vapor barrier systems) can go a long way toward controlling moisture and possible mold problems in homes. The following is a list of general techniques to help control moisture

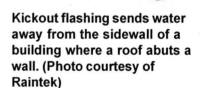

- Direct downspout discharge well away from the foundation.
- Grade away from the house a minimum of 6 inches in the first 10 feet.
- Learn where seasonal high ground water occurs, and do not build basement slabs, floor slabs, or crawlspace floors less than 1 foot above high groundwater (or install a fail-safe pumping system).
- Footing drains should drain to daylight, a drywell, or a sump pump.

Kickout flashing sends water away from the sidewall of a building where a roof abuts a wall. (Photo courtesy of Raintek)

- Install a puncture-resistant polyethylene vapor retarder directly beneath a floor slab.
- Install a capillary moisture break between the top of the footing and the foundation wall (or under a footing that is integral with the slab).
- Install a gravel bed below slab-on-grade floors.
- Use "rainscreen" cladding in all cases where sealing at the surface cannot be guaranteed to stop all water.
- Use kickout flashing where an eave runs into a sidewall.
- Avoid valleys and keep chimneys, dormers, and skylights away from valleys.
- Use substantial crickets where water might not flow easily off the roof.

Walls and Floors

Along with dimension lumber, there are many new and innovative engineered wood products that are finding success in traditional lumber markets. Engineered wood products are made by gluing wood veneer or strands that are graded prior to manufacturing. This results in products which are virtually defect-free with improved structural performance. For example, plywood sheathing has been replaced by OSB sheathing in nearly every part of the country. Another alternative is steel framing, which is light in weight, straight, and unaffected by moisture.

A third is structural masonry, poured-in-place concrete, or precast concrete. All these options are discussed in Chapter 7, Materials.

Other alternatives to conventional wall construction include structural insulated panels (SIPs), where typically a layer of expanded polystyrene (EPS) foam is sandwiched between two layers of OSB, and insulating concrete forms (ICF), where concrete is poured into EPS foam forms that stay in place to create a tightly sealed, well-insulated wall.

Floors made with I-joists or metal-plate connected trusses, have many advantages in addition to their green attributes. By allowing ductwork and piping to run through them, they encourage the practice of keeping ducts and pipes inside the conditioned envelope.

Framing Efficiency

Efficient framing techniques require fewer materials and generate less waste during construction. Rough framing accounts for about 15% to 20% of the total cost of typical home construction. Using proven techniques to reduce the amount of framing material can lower costs, better utilize resources, and save labor.

Optimum value engineering (OVE). OVE or advanced framing uses engineering principles to minimize material usage while meeting model building code structural performance requirements. OVE techniques include the following:

- Increasing wall stud spacing to 24 inches on-center, rather than the standard 16 inches
- Spacing floor joists and roof rafters at 24 inches instead of 16 inches
- Using in-line framing when floor, wall, and roof framing members are in line with one another—sometimes called "in-line" or "stack" framing (in this manner, loads are transferred directly from one bearing member to the next, thus creating a direct load path and a more efficient structure)
- Designing homes on 2-foot modules, thereby reducing waste and installation labor, since most panel products come in even-incremented dimensions such as 4 x 8
- Using two-stud corner framing instead of three studs, and replacing two- and three-stud backing for drywall attachments at wall 'T' intersections with inexpensive drywall clips or scrap lumber
- Properly sizing headers, such as using doubled 2 x 4s, 6s, and 8s over smaller door and window openings instead of doubled 2 x 10s
- Eliminating structural headers in nonloadbearing walls

Substitute 2 x 6 for conventional 2 x 4 framing. 2 x 6 framing at 24" on-center uses roughly the same amount of board-feet of lumber as 2 x 4 lumber at 16" on-center, while leaving a larger wall cavity for increased insulation levels. Once framing crews have gained experience, these techniques can save money by using fewer pieces and being faster to assemble.

Wall Cladding/Exterior Surfaces

Wall cladding (siding) needs to be installed and flashed to manage rainwater. Water typically penetrates through the outer cladding, either by suction (capillary action) or at joints and cracks. More commonly, the outer cladding sheds most of the water, but the real surface that must be sealed from rain occurs at an inner layer that is separated from the outer cladding by an air space. This technique is called "rainscreen" construction. Typical examples of walls that can be built with a rainscreen include wood clapboard, vinyl siding, and EIFS. In the last case, failures of caulking around windows led to the development of rainscreen EIFS designs. Even if you don't install the "rainscreen" drainage space, all walls should be built with a complete drainage layer. In rainscreen or conventional wall construction, the inner water-resistant barrier (building paper or housewrap) must be carefully flashed around all penetrations, especially around windows and doors. A very important technique is to install a "flashing pan" under all windows. There are new peel-and-stick flashing materials that make this task easier.

Roofs

Whether a roof is framed or is trussed, and whether roofing is asphalt, metal, or tile, there are principles that should be followed to minimize the chances of failure leading to water intrusion. Rainwater collects in valleys, and these concentrations increase the chances for water to run up under the roofing at those locations. If you have valleys in the roof, make sure water can flow unimpeded for several feet on either side of the valley. Don't place a dormer or chimney in or near the valley, and don't place dormers close together. When there is an obstruction such as a chimney, or where a "blind" valley occurs between two parallel roofs, there needs to be a substantial cricket that directs water around the obstruction or out of the blind valley. Where an eave ends against a wall, kick-out flashing is needed to prevent water that runs down the joint between wall and roof from penetrating and running behind the siding below.

The living space should be carefully air sealed from the attic or cathedral ceiling to prevent warm, humid interior air from wetting the roof structure in cold weather. Roof ventilation is another topic under intense scrutiny by the building science community, with the final word on the subject yet to be decided. Investigators are experimenting with various methods of reducing attic duct losses or gains: burying the ducts under attic insulation, insulating the home directly under the roof and at the gable end walls, or building a sealed duct plenum into the truss structure. Trusses are widely used in home building. They have the green advantage of using small-dimension and short lengths of lumber. Light-colored asphalt shingles or shiny light-colored painted metal or glazed tile roofing can help reduce attic temperatures.

Insulation and Air Sealing

There are many types of insulation available to the builder, some of which are described in Chapter 7, Materials. Some building systems, such as SIPs, insulating concrete forms (ICFs), and shallow frost-protected foundations (SFPF) include insulation as an integral part of the system. In the open cavities of framed walls, there are many choices.

Fiber Glass Insulation. Fiber glass insulation has natural fire resistance and generally has 20-25% recycled content, including both post-industrial glass cullet and post-consumer recycled bottles. Some products go up to 40% recycled content. These levels meet the EPA Buying Guidelines in terms of recycled content. Fiber glass is made from glass cullet and sand, which are widely available, rapidly renewable resources, and uses minimal packaging. Fiber glass insulation is used in walls, ceilings, and cavities in the form of batts, blankets, and loose fill.

State-of-the-art soft foam insulation is sprayed into walls, floors, and ceilings.

Many manufacturers have certified their products to the GREENGUARD® specification, and fiber glass products are available with or without formaldehyde binders. The Consumer Products Safety Commission has concluded that the amount of formaldehyde present in fiber glass is not a concern. See Chapter 6, Indoor Environmental Quality, for more information on air sealing and duct work.

Vapor Retarders

Humidity in the air can move through ordinary building materials by a process called vapor diffusion. In the past 50 years, a strong emphasis on vapor diffusion as a source of moisture problems in wall, attics, and cathedral ceilings has led to the almost universal requirement for a strongly effective vapor retarder. Recently, this emphasis has been re-examined in light of condensation problems in air-conditioned homes in hot–humid climates, where an interior vapor retarder contributes to the moisture problems rather than solving them.

Air and water leakage, not diffusion, are the primary causes of moisture damage in walls and attics. Once air leakage is controlled by air sealing and water leakage is controlled by proper water management techniques, the vapor retarder can be chosen to suit a specific climate.

Look for climate-specific improvements in the vapor retarder requirements of the national model codes, starting with the 2008 International Residential Code (IRC).

Cellulose Loose-Fill Insulation. Cellulose loose-fill insulation is made from wastepaper, such as used newsprint and boxes, that is shredded and pulverized into small fibrous particles. Chemicals are then added to provide resistance to fire and insects. In many cases, cellulose is labeled with both "settled thickness" and "installed thickness." To ensure thermal performance, it is essential to follow the manufacturer's guidance for installed thickness, so that proper R-value is achieved. Loose-fill insulation can be easier to fit around pipes and other obstructions in a wall assembly. Cellulose is sometimes applied in a wetspray form. Care should be taken to allow for appropriate drying time based on both temperature and humidity levels.

Mineral Wool Insulation. When installing insulation to a high-temperature surface, mineral wool is ideal. It is also used as passive fire protection. Mineral wool comes in board, blanket and loose fill forms. Many types of mineral wool insulation have recycled content as high as 70%. Slag wool insulation contains as much as 90% recycled blast furnace slag, some of which is reclaimed from landfills for use in insulation.

Other Insulation Products. Besides the very common batts and rolls of fiber glass, there are batts made of cotton or rock wool. Cellulose, fiber glass, and rock wool can all be sprayed into open wall cavities. If not allowed to dry thoroughly before enclosing, wet-applied products may support mold growth and damage other building materials with which they come into contact. If the cavities are covered by netting or polyethylene, aerated dry material can be blown in.

Foam-in-place insulation is typically either high-density or low-density polyurethane. Foam can be sprayed directly into cavities, either filling them or creating an air-sealing liner over which batts can be placed. Foams have the advantage that they can be sprayed into overhead cavities, creating an air-sealed cocoon around the living space, and can be used to create unvented attic and cathedral ceiling spaces (according to the 2004 and 2006 IRC), or to insulate roof lines that cannot be properly vented. They can also be sprayed directly on concrete or masonry. Because foam can be more expensive to install, a hybrid system in which foam is applied to the sheathing and then covered with a fiber glass batt can be an alternative. However, care must be taken to prevent condensation within the wall. Where rigid board is needed, polyisocyanurate is available with impervious skins on both sides, while unfaced expanded polystyrene (EPS) and extruded polystyrene (XPS) are both widely available in a variety of thicknesses and sizes.

CFC-Free Spray Foam Insulation. Foam insulation has excellent air-sealing qualities, moisture resistance, and insulating properties. Choose foam insulation products that use a lower ozone-depleting blowing agent such as HCFCs (hydrochlorofluorocarbons), HFCs (hydrofluorocarbons), or better yet, CO_2, pentane, and isobutene.

Exposed or Unexposed? When installing insulation materials in occupied or unoccupied spaces, be aware of the building code requirements for flame spread and smoke-developed indices. These code requirements will dictate whether materials such as vapor retarders and insulation can be left exposed or must be covered by a fire-resistive barrier, or an "ignition" barrier in the case of a cathedralized attic where access is required for service of HVAC equipment.

Air Leakage Driving Forces

Requirements for air leakage to occur are:

1. *Holes.* The larger the hole, the greater the air leakage. Large holes have higher priority for air sealing efforts.
2. *Driving force.* A pressure difference that forces air to flow through a hole. Holes that experience stronger and more continuous driving forces have higher priority.

The common driving forces are:

1. *Wind.* Caused by weather conditions.
2. *Stack effect.* Upward air pressure due to the buoyancy of air.
3. *Mechanical blower.* Induced pressure imbalances caused by operation of fans and blowers.

Wind is usually considered to be the primary driving force for air leakage, but in most locations wind is intermittent and relatively minor. When the wind blows against a building, it creates a high pressure zone on the windward areas. Outdoor air from the windward side infiltrates into the building while air exits on the leeward side. Wind acts to create areas of differential pressure, which cause both infiltration and exfiltration. The degree to which wind contributes to air leakage depends on its velocity and duration.

The temperature difference between inside and outside causes warm air inside the home to rise creating a driving force known as the *stack effect.* Cold air is drawn in at the bottom of the structure to replace the warm air that escapes near the top. In homes with large holes in the attic and crawlspace or basement, the stack effect can be a major contributor to air leakage, moisture, and air quality problems.

Poorly designed and installed forced-air systems can create strong pressure imbalances inside the home whenever the heating and cooling system operates. In addition, unsealed ductwork located in attics and crawlspaces can draw pollutants and excess moisture into the home. Correcting duct leakage problems is critical when constructing an energy-efficient home.

Wind Driven Infiltration

On average, wind in the Southeast creates a pressure difference of 10 to 20 Pascals on the windward side. However, most homes have only small cracks on the exterior.

The Stack Effect

The stack effect can create pressure differences between 1 to 3 Pascals due to the power of rising warm air. Crawl space and attic holes are often large.

Mechanical System Driven Infiltration

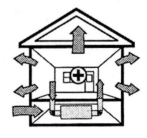

Leaks in supply and return ductwork can cause pressure differences of up to 30 Pascals. Exhaust equipment such as kitchen and bath fans and clothes dryers can also create pressure differences.

Air Infiltration Control

This is a brief overview of the many infiltration issues that arise when constructing an energy-efficient house. Sealing the house carefully to reduce air infiltration is as necessary as adding insulation. Consider the following:

- In cold climates, it is generally safe to wrap the inside of a home that is *not air conditioned* with most types of "vapor retarders."
- The preferred strategy for an air conditioned home in a cold climate is to caulk every leakage path and use a moderately effective vapor retarder, such as the kraft paper facing on batt insulation or vapor retarder paint (primer).
- In hot and humid climates, it is essential to avoid any sort of vapor retarder on the inside surface (including vinyl wallpaper) to reduce condensation so that when the wall or ceiling gets wet, it can dry out to the air conditioned interior.
- In all climates, make sure all wall cavities are well sealed to minimize air leakage, or fill the cavity with sprayed-on insulation. When using damp-spray cellulose, take measurements to ensure that it has dried out before applying interior finishes.
- Be certain to use sealants that are adequately flexible and can bridge the gap. Larger openings should be sealed with rigid materials, using caulk or foam around the perimeter.
- Perform air sealing to control infiltration at the most common sources: floor-wall junctions (sillplates), wall outlets, windows and window openings, HVAC ducts, fireplaces, recessed lighting fixtures (see Chapter 4, Energy Efficiency), and exterior venting devices for bathrooms, kitchens, and laundry rooms. Careful caulking in these areas will reduce infiltration and control moisture. The cost of air sealing to a moderate level of about 0.3 ach natural is between $250 and $500.
- Installing house wrap or building paper as air barriers over the exterior sheathing can reduce air leakage and moisture penetration. Ensure proper installation by taping all seams and wrapping and/or taping at penetrations such as windows, doors, vents, etc. Most of the largest leaks in homes occur where framing (such as floor joists or wall studs) span from an area inside conditioned space to an unconditioned or vented space, such as attic, garage, or roof.

See "Gap Sealing Checklist for Homes" on the next page for details of where and how to gap seal.

Air Infiltration Control Checklist

Typical Home Air Leakage Sites

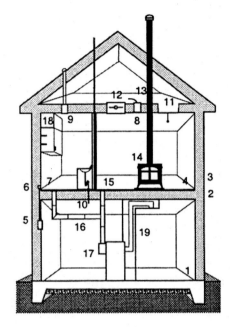

1. *Slab floors:* Seal all holes in the slab to prevent entry of water vapor and soil gas. A vapor retarder beneath the slab will reduce water vapor transmissions and help control indoor relative humidity levels.

2. *Sill plate and rim joist:* Seal sill plates in basements and unvented crawlspaces. Caulk or gasket rim or band joists between floors in multi-story construction.

3. *Bottom plate:* Use either caulk or gasket between the plate and subflooring.

4. *Subfloor:* Use an adhesive to seal the seams between pieces of subflooring.

5. *Electrical wiring:* Use wire-compatible caulk or spray foam to seal penetrations.

6. *Electrical boxes:* Use approved caulk to seal wiring on the outside of electrical boxes. Seal between the interior finish material and boxes.

7. *Electrical box gaskets:* Caulk foam gaskets to all electrical boxes in exterior and interior walls before installing coverplates.

8. *Recessed light fixtures:* Consider using surface-mounted light fixtures rather than recessed lights. When used, specify airtight models rated for insulation coverage (IC).

9. *Exhaust fans:* Seal between the fan housing and the interior finish material. Choose products with tight-fitting backdraft dampers.

10. *Plumbing:* Locate plumbing in interior walls, and minimize penetrations. Seal all penetrations with foam sealant or caulk.

11. *Attic access:* Weatherstrip attic access openings. For pull-down stairs, use latches to hold the door panel tightly against the weatherstripping. Cover the attic access opening with an insulated box.

12. *Whole house fan:* Use a panel made of rigid insulation or plastic to seal the interior louvers when not in use.

13. *Flue stacks:* Install a code-approved flue collar and seal with fire-rated caulk.

14. *Combustion appliances:* Closely follow local codes for firestopping measures, which reduce air leakage as well as increase the safety of the appliance. Make certain all combustion appliances, such as stoves and fireplaces, have an outside source of combustion air and tight-fitting dampers or doors.

15. *Return and supply registers:* Seal all boots connected to registers or grilles to the interior finish material.

16. *Ductwork:* Seal all joints in supply and return duct systems with mastic.

17. *Air handling unit* (for heating and cooling system): Seal all cracks and unnecessary openings with mastic. Seal service panels with tape.

18. *Dropped ceiling soffit:* Use sheet material and sealant to stop air leakage from attic into the soffit or wall framing, then insulate.

19. *Chases* (for ductwork, flues, etc.): Prevent air leakage through these bypasses with sheet materials and sealants.

Air Infiltration Control Diagrams

Sealing Bypasses

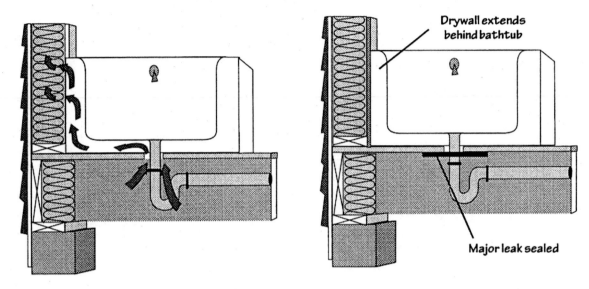

Drywall extends behind bathtub

Major leak sealed

Plumbing - Seal penetrations, especially under bathtubs and other fixtures. Install drywall, plastic, or housewrap behind bathtub to provide an air barrier.

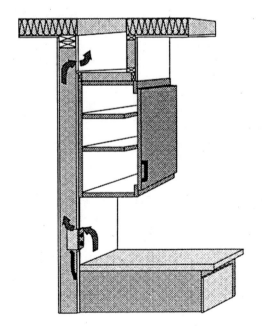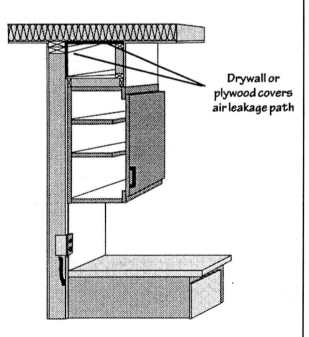

Drywall or plywood covers air leakage path

Dropped Ceiling Soffit - If kitchen cabinets or bath/shower enclosures have dropped soffits, provide a continuous seal at the attic floor.

Air Infiltration Control Diagrams (continued)

Sealing Bypasses for Flues and Ductwork

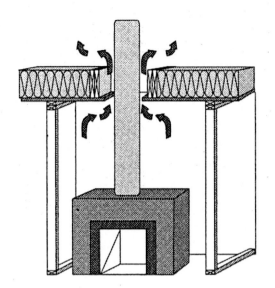
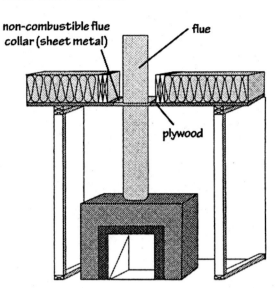

Chases - Framed chases for flues should be sealed at the attic floor. Use a continuous layer of plywood or other solid sheet-good. Seal between the flue and combustible materials with fire-rated caulk and a noncombustible flue collar.

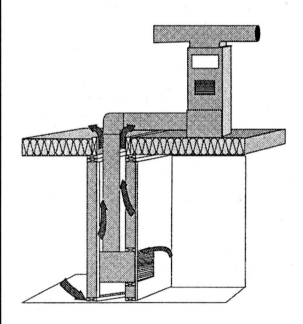
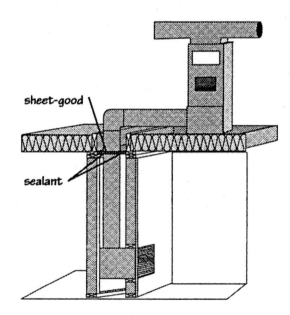

Return and Supply Plenums - Seal framed areas for ductwork.

Windows

Windows play a crucial role in creating an energy-efficient envelope. How they are installed and flashed is crucial to maintaining the moisture integrity of the walls, as discussed above. Flashing around windows should carefully overlap the upper layer over the lower one in all cases. Do not rely upon window flanges set in sealant to keep water out, and use flashing pans whenever possible. References are given that describe proper window flashing in detail.

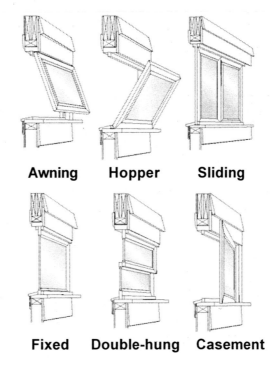

Awning   Hopper   Sliding

Fixed   Double-hung   Casement

Energy-efficient windows come in traditional styles.

The Building Envelope — Rules of Thumb

- Consider advanced framing to reduce framing costs, add strength to a home's envelope, and reduce material consumption.
- Pay careful attention to water movement and vapor movement.
- Install a "flashing pan" under all windows.
- Use the "Gap Sealing Checklist" for your homes.
- Stay abreast of rapidly changing building science and codes regarding crawlspace and roof ventilation and vapor retarders.
- Consider advanced foundation systems such as FPSFs and ICFs.

Additional Resources

Builder's Guide: Hot–Dry and Mixed–Dry Climates. Office of Building Technology, State and Community Programs, Energy Efficiency and Renewable Energy, U.S. Department of Energy. 2000.

"Advanced Wall Framing," *Technology Fact Sheet,* Office of Building Technology, State and Community Programs, Energy Efficiency and Renewable Energy, U.S. Department of Energy. October 2000. 800-DOE-3732; www.eere.energy.gov/

GreenSpec: The Environmental Building News Product Directory and Guideline Specifications, Dwight Homes, Larry Strain, AIA, Alex Wilson, and Sandra Leibowitz. BuildingGreen, Inc., Brattleboro, Vermont. 4th Edition. www.greenspec.com

Guide to Resource Efficient Building Elements, Mumma, Tracy. National Center for Appropriate Technology's Center for Resourceful Building Technology, Missoula, Montana. www.crbt.org

Building Greener Building Better, The National Association of Home Builders and the NAHB Research Center, Washington, D.C. 2002.

Water Management Guide, Lstiburek, Joseph W., EEBA, Inc., Minneapolis, MN.

Web Resources

www.efficientwindows.org
    U.S. Department of Energy: Efficient Windows Collaborative
www.pathnet.org
www.toolbase.org
www.ecco.org
    The Environmental Council of Concrete Organizations provides bulletins on using concrete as part of a sustainable environment. 800-994-3226
www.greenbuilder.com/sourcebook/
    The city of Austin's Green Building Network materials sourcebook.
www.nfrc.org
    The National Fenestration Ratings Council Web site provides an industry-standard rating for use by manufacturers. Helpful window selection information is also available.
www.eere.energy.gov
    For information on topics related to this chapter, search U.S. DOE's Energy-Efficiency and Renewable Energy Office web pages
www.ornl.gov/sci/roofs+walls/insulation.ins_01.html
    Insulation Fact Sheet, Oak Ridge National Laboratory Building Research Program
www.naima.org
    The North American Insulation Manufacturers Association
www.cima.org
    The Cellulose Insulation Manufacturers Association

www.concretethinker.com and www.concretehome.com
Portland Cement Association information on concrete and sustainability
www.forms.org
Insulating Concrete Form Association
www.greenguard.org
Greenguard Environmental Institute

Interactions

See the following sections for information on how The Building Envelope affects other building considerations:

Chapter 4   Energy Efficiency

HEATING AND AIR CONDITIONING SYSTEMS

Heating and cooling can use over 40% of a home's energy. In cold climates, heating alone can account for as much as two thirds of a home's energy consumption. Designing, selecting, and installing more efficient, properly sized HVAC systems will keep your home buyers comfortable and happy while saving them money. Using better design and construction techniques can reduce material and installation costs while reducing the homeowner's energy bill. (Note that the efficiency of all the systems described depends on regular maintenance.) Efficient duct system design, correct register placement, duct layout, duct sealing, and insulation can account for HVAC efficiency gains of up to 30%.

Ductwork Versus No Ductwork

The type of heating and air conditioning system and equipment needed depends on whether the home has been designed with or without ductwork. If air conditioning is required, a home will need ductwork to distribute cool air. This chapter touches on ductwork design and detailing. The existence of ductwork automatically tilts the decision concerning how to heat a home in favor of warm air heating, because the cost of the system for distributing heat is already incorporated in the system for distributing cool air. However, it is possible at extra cost to add a separate heating system, either radiant baseboards or wall units, or increasingly, radiant piping in the floor. The typical argument in favor of a separate system is that cool air is ideally distributed near the ceiling, while heating is better delivered near floor level, but this rationale is not valid when good design principles are followed.

Heating System Options

Baseboard or other radiators. In climates where air conditioning is not required, baseboard radiators are a common form of heating. Attractive radiant wall panels are available, widely used in Europe, that do not interfere with furniture placement. Baseboard units can be either sheet metal or cast iron. Cast iron units, while more expensive, provide considerable mass that evens out the flow of heat and reduces short-cycling. One great advantage of radiator systems is that they are easily zoned. Zoning of heating is a green strategy because seldom-used spaces can be kept cooler, thus saving energy. The equipment used to generate heat in a radiator heating system is always a boiler or a water heater.

Radiant floor systems. Radiant floor heating using in-the-floor piping is an old technology with a history of failure due to leakage and corrosion of metal piping. With the development of "PEX" (cross-linked polyethylene) tubing, radiant floor heating has become reliably free from leakage. Its well-known comfort advantages have renewed its popularity across the country. Typically, the tubing is cast into light-weight concrete fill, to reduce the weight. However, in a passive solar heated home, it is important that the fill be normal weight to enhance its mass storage capacity (see Chapter 2, Renewable Energy, "Passive Solar Design Strategies"). It is also possible to install radiant heating under wood floors.

Radiant floor systems, like radiator systems, are easily zoned, using a central manifold. A boiler or water heater is typically used to generate heat in a radiant floor heating. In some cases, because of the low water temperature used, it is possible to use a ground-source heat pump to generate the needed warm water. However, a boiler or water heater booster will be necessary to deal with the coldest weather. Whether radiant floor heating saves energy relative to radiators or warm-air heating is controversial. What is not controversial is that radiant floor heating, properly designed, is very comfortable and highly desired by homeowners. Costs vary from $2.00/SF for systems installed as part of a planned concrete slab, up to $6.00/SF for thin-plate systems (used under wood flooring decks).

Warm air systems. While ducted warm air heating is the obvious choice for an air conditioned home, even without air conditioning it is a popular option. It is often less expensive than a hydronic system (one using warm or hot water to heat space directly) and if properly designed, can deliver excellent comfort. Poorly designed hot air systems have a bad reputation in cold climates because they are noisy and blow excessively hot air at high velocities. Good design avoids these problems. Ducted warm air systems allow easy humidification (but see concerns about excess humidity) and filtering. They also avoid the protruding baseboard or other radiators used in hydronic systems. A major advantage of warm air heating is that the system can be installed initially without air conditioning, which can easily be added later if the owner desires.

The heating equipment used with warm-air heating is typically a gas furnace, which heats the air directly. A furnace consists of a fan and filter, the combustion chamber, the heat exchanger, and if air conditioning is present, the air conditioning coil. All this equipment without the combustion chamber is called an air handler. Less commonly, heat can be generated in a furnace by electric resistance coils (often the choice in climates with very mild winters), or by burning oil.

Two other heating equipment options are available. One is a heat pump, which uses the cooling coil in an air handler to deliver heat (essentially an air conditioner that "runs backwards"), usually with electric resistance backup heat. The other option is to generate hot water with a boiler or water heater and to circulate this water through a coil in the air handler that replaces the furnace as the source of heat. This "hydro air" option is an attractive one and is discussed below.

Any ducted system is difficult to zone. If zoning is desired and the budget allows, a separate unit can be provided for each zone. Another option is to use distributed "hydro-air" fan-coil units.

Hydro air systems. As noted previously, it is possible to use a heating coil in an air handler to create warm air for distribution through ductwork. Such a system brings with it many advantages:

- If the hot water is generated with a boiler, the same boiler can also be used to generate domestic hot water (at high efficiency).
- If the heating load is small, the water heater can produce the hot water.
- Hot water can be used simultaneously to heat air, to heat radiators, and, at a reduced temperature, to heat radiant floors.
- Water can easily be moved to remote locations in the home through piping, keeping hot elements inside the conditioned envelope of the home.

Typical hydro air systems (those that heat and cool air using water) include the following:

1. *Heating by water heater.* In climates with mild winters and in low-energy buildings in any climate, hot water from a standard or high-efficiency water heater can be used to heat the air for the ducted warm air heating system. A packaged coil and pump is available for this purpose. A high-efficiency sealed combustion water heater is a good choice for such a system. The water heater should always be sealed-combustion or power-vented to eliminate a potential source of pollution from backdrafting. Some code jurisdictions require a heat exchanger in order to allow the use of the domestic water heater for space heating.

2. *Heating by boiler.* A high-efficiency boiler can be used both to feed a coil in an air handler and to heat domestic water. Instead of a water heater, a pump circulates hot water from the boiler to an insulated storage tank. Because the tank does not have a flue, it is a more efficient way to store hot water than in a typical water heater. The domestic water storage tank can be remotely located near the point of use, eliminating the water and energy loss associated with drawing hot water from a distance.

Air Conditioning System Options

A "mini-duct" system, which uses higher system pressure to move air through very small ducts, has the great advantage that ductwork can snake through smaller openings within the framing, making it easier to keep the ductwork within the conditioned envelope. Such a system is also very useful in renovations. Heating in a mini-duct system is accomplished by a hydro air coil fed by a boiler or water heater.

The ductwork found in central air conditioning systems can be zoned, but this requires motorized dampers, dump zones, and complex controls. A more reliable choice for larger and more expensive homes is to serve each area with its own individual air conditioning system. However, the best choice for most air-conditioned "green" homes is to avoid zoning. Zoning is less important as the space-cooling loads are reduced. This approach reduces the possibility that underserved areas might accumulate excess amounts of humidity. In humid climates, an essential function of air conditioning is dehumidification, so every space needs to be served.

Evaporative Coolers

Evaporative coolers, or "swamp coolers," can be effective in dry climates, but in general use large amounts of water. In humid weather, however, they are not at all effective, and they are vulnerable to the hard water that is common in dry climates. Unlike all other space conditioning systems, evaporative coolers introduce and exhaust large amounts of outside air, automatically providing extensive ventilation. If pollen is a problem, effective filtration of the incoming air is a necessity.

Sizing and Designing Systems

Use Manual J and Manual S (published by the Air Conditioning Contractors of America) or other similar resources to properly size your HVAC units. Do not rely on rules of thumb, such as 600 square feet of cooled area per ton of air conditioning. (A well-designed home may need only a ton for every 1,000 SF.) Oversized units perform inefficiently and can create uncomfortable conditions, especially during cooling cycles. Rather than oversizing the units, carefully design the HVAC system to be the proper size as a way of reducing callbacks. Consider low window SHGC ratings, natural ventilation, reduced internal gains, passive solar heating and cooling load reductions, ceiling fans, energy-efficient appliances, and other green building attributes in your calculations. Before and during construction, be sure to adjust calculations for design changes that impact heating and cooling loads (and inform HVAC subcontractors of those changes).

Heating and Air Conditioning Systems – Rules of Thumb

- Do not use rules of thumb for sizing HVAC units.
- Perform Manual J sizing calculations and Manual S for equipment selection or use similar resources.
- Consider radiant floor heating for added comfort and efficiency.
- Multiple thermostats/zones may offer a cost-effective way to heat and cool larger homes.

Manual J Example*

Manual J, Load Calculation for Residential Winter and Summer Air Conditioning, is published by the Air Conditioning Contractors of America (ACCA.) The procedures in the manual calculate the building heating and cooling loads as follows:

1. Determine all dimensions of the exterior building envelope for each type of surface (wall, floor, window, door, ceiling, etc.)

2. Note R-values of all components.

3. Find the Construction Number of each component based on tables in the book.

4. Look up climatic data in the manual for the locality in which the home is being constructed.

5. Based on the Construction Number and the climatic data, find the Heat Transfer Multiplier (HTM) for the different components during the heating (Htg.) and cooling (Clg.) seasons.

6. Fill in the tables for the heating and cooling load.

7. Calculate the infiltration loads, internal gains, and latent loads in separate charts.

8. Find the grand total loads.

9. Use *Manual S, Residential Equipment Selection*, also published by ACCA, to help select the equipment for the home.

1	Name of Room				Entire House		
2	Running Ft. Exposed Wall				94.5		
3	Room Dimensions Ft.			32	62.5		
4	Ceiling Ht. Ft.				8		

	TYPE OF EXPOSURE		Const. No.	HTM Htg.	HTM Clg.	Area/ Length	Btuh Htg.	Btuh Clg.
5	Gross Exposed Walls & Partitions	a b c d	12F				1,512	
6	Windows & Glass Doors Htg.	a b c d	3b	30.5		300	9,150	
7	Windows & Glass Doors Clg.	North E&W South			16 46 25	75 150 75		1,200 6,900 1,875
8	Other Doors		10D	23	10.9	42	966	458
9	Net Exposed Walls & Partitions	a b c d	12F	3.5	1.7	1,170	4,095	1,989
10	Ceilings	a b	16G	1.6	1.2	2,000	3,200	2,400
11	Floors	a b	19D	1.3	0	2,000	2,600	0
12	Infiltration HTM						11,757	5,878
13	Sub Total Btuh Loss = 6+8+9+10+11+12						31,768	20,700
14	Duct Btuh Loss		0.1				3,177	0
15	**Total Btuh Loss = 13 + 14**						34,945	
16	People @ 300 & Appliances= 1200							2,400
17	Sensible Btuh Gain = 7+8+9+10+11+12+16							23,100
18	Duct Btuh Gain		0.05					1,155
19	**Total Sensible Gain**							24,255
	Latent Gain Calculations							
	Latent Infiltration							2,471
	Latent Ventilation							0
	Latent Internal Gains							1,920
	Total Latent Gain							4,391

* A *Manual J* calculation takes approximately 30 to 60 minutes for an average home. The measurements for the calculations are available from the construction drawings. *Manual S* calculations require an additional 15 to 30 minutes.

Additional Resources

A Builder's Guide to Residential HVAC Systems, NAHB Research Center, Home Builder Press. 1997. Provides extensive information about HVAC sizing, design, and equipment selection, and also includes energy-efficiency considerations.

A Builder's Guide to Energy Efficient Homes in Georgia, Southface Energy Institute, Inc. Offers excellent descriptions and diagrams of different HVAC systems. Lots of information on sizing, installation, and duct work.

Air Conditioning Contractors of America offers *Manuals J & S* and other information to help builders size and design their HVAC systems. www.acca.org

Portland Cement Association offers *HVAC Sizing for Concrete Homes* software to help builders size and design their HVAC systems. www.cement.org

Web Resources

www.ashrae.org
   American Society of Heating, Refrigeration, and Air-Conditioning Engineers, Inc.
www.toolbase.org/ToolbaseResources
   Toolbase Services: Heating, Ventilating, and Air Conditioning
www.eere.energy.gov/buildings/info/homes/coolinghome.html
   U.S. Department of Energy: Heating and Cooling Your Home

Interactions

See the following sections for information on how Heating and Air Conditioning Systems affect other building considerations:

HEATING AND AIR CONDITIONING EQUIPMENT

Air Conditioning Equipment

A typical residential air conditioning equipment package consists of a condensing unit, placed outside the house, and an evaporator coil inside, located in the air handler or furnace. Heat pumps, natural ventilation, and other alternatives are also proven, reliable ways to cool homes in many climates.

Right-size whatever equipment is chosen for the home to save on costs and to create greater comfort (see discussion of Manual J sizing in the previous section, "Heating and Air Conditioning Systems"). Even conservatively oversized air conditioners cost more to purchase, and create humidity problems, by cycling off before they have a chance to dehumidify the air. This is uncomfortable for the homeowner and, if serious enough, may contribute to diminished indoor environmental quality. Oversized units are also poor energy performers. Include natural ventilation, shading from overhangs and landscaping, and ceiling fan effects in your calculations.

Select central air conditioning units with an ENERGY STAR® rating. ENERGY STAR® air conditioners are at least 20% more efficient than standard equipment and have a Seasonal Energy Efficiency Rating (SEER) of 14 or higher. The SEER rating is usually shown on the yellow and black EnergyGuide sticker attached to the unit's exterior.

A final consideration is noise. Some homeowners find that the noise created by a condensing unit outside can interfere with indoor or outdoor peace and quiet. Air conditioners are rated on a scale of 0 to 13 bels (a bel is 10 decibels). Most air conditioners and heat pumps operate in the range of 8 to 9 bels, although some units are as quiet as 6.8 bels. Units with variable speed fans are among the quietest (see below). Noise can also be transmitted directly through the electrical conduit and tubing to the house wall from a condenser placed close to the house.

Variable Speed Units

Units with multi-speed compressors and with variable speed indoor fans are more efficient than conventional units. They can achieve SEER ratings of up to 21, but at a higher cost than standard units. Added advantages include quieter operation and better dehumidification.

Heat Pumps

Heat pumps both heat and cool homes. See the following "Heating Equipment" section for more tips on heat pumps.

Heating Equipment

Residential boiler or furnace efficiency is measured by annual fuel utilization efficiency (AFUE). AFUE is a measure of how efficiently the appliance uses fuel (oil or gas) over the course of a typical year. Although condensing units cost more than noncondensing units, selecting a condensing fossil-fueled furnace or boiler may be a good choice in areas with high heating costs. The AFUE of conventional equipment is limited to approximately 80%. Above this efficiency, flue gasses condense and corrode the equipment. Once this limit is breached with condensing appliances, they are typically designed for 90-95% AFUE. Vents are typically 2" PVC piping, exiting through the sidewall, and the units draw in their own combustion air through another PVC pipe (they are "sealed combustion" appliances). There may be restrictions regarding the proximity of vents to door and window openings, the length of run, and the number of bends. See the "Combustion Safety" section in Chapter 6, Indoor Environmental Quality, for more information on how to mitigate indoor air hazards (such as backdrafting) through proper design and installation of combustion appliances.

If electricity is the only fuel source for heating, a heat pump (air or ground-source) system or zoned electric resistance system should be considered. Central electric furnaces or boilers will be expensive to operate, unless the heating season is brief. Heat pumps are more efficient. Zoned electric baseboards or wall heaters (with their own thermostats) allow you to provide heat only when and where it is desired. There are minimal distribution system losses. Conventional programmable thermostats are not compatible with heat pumps; use special programmable thermostats designed specifically for heat pumps.

Geothermal Heat Pumps

Also called ground source heat pumps, geothermal units heat and cool the home by using the constant temperature of the earth as a source of heat in the winter and as a heat sink during the summer. The performance of geothermal heat pumps is typically better than air-source heat pumps, with Coefficients of Performance (COP) typically in the range of 3.5 to 4.5. These values translate into SEER ratings of 14 to 19. Select units with an ENERGY STAR® label. Note that some units may use the Heating Season Performance Factor (HSPF) rather than COP. Select a unit with an HSPF rating of 9 or higher. Other advantages include their long life expectancy (25 years) and their ability to deliver hot water at a greater efficiency than standard electric water heaters. Disadvantages include higher first costs ($1,000 to $1,500 per ton higher than conventional HVAC) and land requirements for horizontal buried pipes for heat transfer (ground source). It is important to consider the power requirements of loop or well pumping in the overall efficiency of the unit. To mitigate land requirements, consider vertical loops. The Geothermal Heat Pump Consortium promotes geothermal heat pumps to builders and home buyers, and some local utilites may offer financial incentives.

Air Source Heat Pumps

These are the most common type of heat pumps and, like the geothermal units, both heat and cool the home. Most heat pumps operate at least twice as effectively as conventional electric resistance heating systems. Air-source heat pumps should have an outdoor thermostat to prevent operation of electrical strip heaters when temperatures climb above 35 or 40 degrees. Some heat pumps are installed with duel-fuel or piggyback systems that heat the home with gas when temperatures drop to the point where the heat pump can no longer meet the heating load of the home, typically below 25 to 35 degrees. Select units with an HSPF of 8.2 or greater, as these meet ENERGY STAR® requirements.

Efficient Duct Design and Installation

Duct leakage constitutes 10% to 30% of heating and cooling loads in many homes. In addition, duct leakage can lessen comfort and endanger health and safety. Make sure your HVAC contractor is, at a minimum, familiar with the design information, products, and installation techniques described below.

The three most common types of duct material used in home construction are metal, fiber glass duct board, and flex duct. Duct work should be insulated if not inside the conditioned space. If the ducts are inside the conditioned space, duct liner helps attenuate sound from the HVAC unit and between rooms. Both metal and fiber glass duct board are rigid and installed in pieces.

Many contractors install a system using all 6-inch duct runs to rooms. However, proper duct size depends on the estimated heating and cooling load for each room in the house, the length, type and shape of the duct, and the operating characteristics of the HVAC system, such as the pressure, temperature, and fan speed. Use *Manual D, Duct Design* published by the Air Conditioning Contractors of America (ACCA) to calculate the proper air flow and duct size for each room.

Efficient Duct Design and Installation Diagrams

Disconnected Ducts Are High Priorities

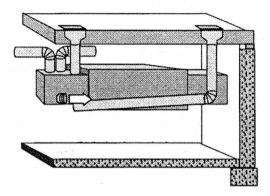

Ducts can become disconnected during initial installation, maintenance, or even normal operation. They should be checked periodically for problems.

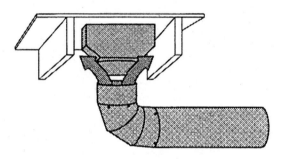

Disconnection at boot

Sometimes, disconnected ducts can be hidden behind the insulation. Look for kinks or curves where there is no elbow.

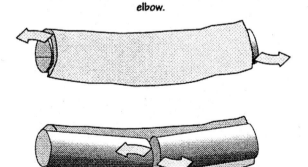

Duct Leaks in Inside Spaces

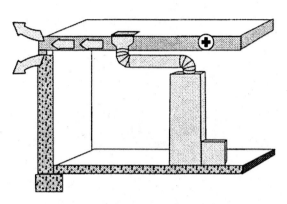

Although this supply duct is theoretically in conditioned space, the supply leaks pressurize the band joist area and air leaks to the outside. The best solution—seal all duct leaks and all building envelope air leaks

Figure 8-4
Seal All Leaks in Air Handling Unit

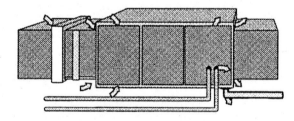

Many air handling cabinets come from the factory with leaks, which should be sealed with duct-sealing mastic. Removable panels should be sealed with tape.

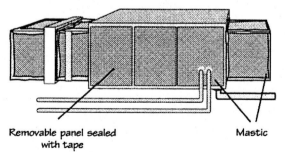

Removable panel sealed with tape   Mastic

Efficient Duct Design and Installation Diagrams (continued)

Shelf-Mounted Systems Without Returns

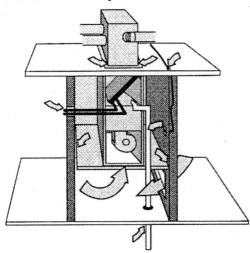

Non-ducted returns can severely depressurize mechanical room closets, not only sapping the system's efficiency, but also creating ideal conditions for backdrafting and other air quality problems. Seal all leaks with mastic or caulk.

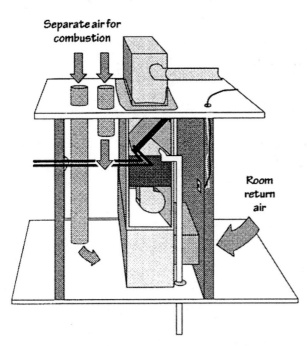

Separate air for combustion

Room return air

The return should be connected to the home via a well sealed duct. All holes from the mechanical room closet to other spaces should be completely sealed.

Seal All Leaky Takeoffs

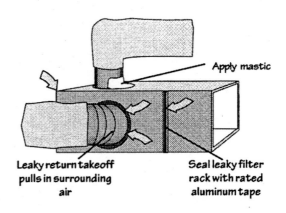

Apply mastic

Leaky return takeoff pulls in surrounding air

Seal leaky filter rack with rated aluminum tape

Figure 8-7
Sealing Leaky Boots

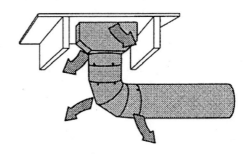

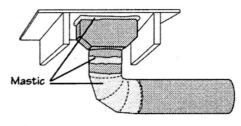

Mastic

Use mastic to completely seal all leaky seams and holes. Use mesh tape with mastic to cover cracks over 1/8-inch wide.

Duct Installation Tips: High-Priority Leaks

High-priority leaks, which should always be sealed with mastic, include the following:

1. Disconnected components, including take-offs that are not fully inserted, plenums or ducts that have been dislodged, tears in flex-duct, and strained connections between ductwork (visible when the duct bends where there is no elbow)
2. The joints between sections of branch ductwork
3. The return take-offs, elbows, boots, and other connections (if the return is built into an interior wall, all connections and seams must be carefully sealed)
4. The take-offs from the main supply plenum or trunk line
5. Any framing in the building used as ductwork, such as a "panned" joist where sheet metal nailed to floor joists provides a space for conditioned air to flow (it is preferable to avoid using framing as a part of the duct system).

In addition, pay careful attention to the connections between the air handling unit and the supply and return plenums. Check all of the seams in the air handling unit, plenums, and rectangular ductwork—particularly underneath components and in any other tight areas. Also seal the holes for the refrigerant, thermostat, and condensate lines. Use tape rather than mastic to seal the seams in the panel of the air handling unit so they can be removed during servicing. After completion of service and maintenance work, such as filter changing, advise the homeowner to make sure the seams are retaped. Lastly, check the connections near the supply registers, between the branch ductwork and the boot, the seams of the elbows, and all other potential leaks in these areas.

Duct Installation Tips: Low-Priority Leaks

Low-priority leaks include the following:

1. Longitudinal seams in round metal ductwork
2. The boot and the register

Additional Duct Design and Installation Recommendations

1. Use only high-quality caulking or foam sealant and duct-sealing water-based mastic with fiber glass mesh (highly preferred). This strategy may add $20 to $55 and one person day to the cost of a $5,000 system, but it will reap energy and dollar savings for the owner.

2. *Never* use duct tape to seal leaks in ductwork.

3. In energy-efficient houses (homes with extra insulation and high-performance windows) it is not necessary to place registers on the outside walls or under or above windows to maintain occupant comfort, as is traditional practice. Locating both supply and return ducts near the core of the house saves builders labor and material costs. Registers may be placed high on sidewalls for best mixing of air in both heating and cooling seasons.

4. Locate ducts within the conditioned space to minimize leakage problems.

5. Use duct insulation of at least R-6 value, and install the vapor retarder to the outside of the insulation facing away from the duct.

6. Round and rectangular metal ducts must be sealed with mastic and insulated during installation. It is important to seal the seams first, because insulation does not stop air leaks.

7. Flex duct has higher pressure losses than those associated with metal duct work. Flex duct is flexible and comes in long sections. If flex duct is used, it is important that the soft lining material of the flex duct not be punctured or torn and that the layout be carefully designed to minimize pressure losses.

8. Minimize use of elbows and sharp turns.

9. Locate registers so that they do not blow air directly onto occupants. This is particularly important when using heat pumps or other moderate temperature heating sources.

10. Locate intake ducts away from exhausts from the laundry, kitchen, chimney, or fireplace.

11. The air-tightness of duct work can be tested after installation using calibrated fans and testing procedures similar to blower door tests.

HVAC Controls: Programmable Thermostats

Programmable thermostats are an inexpensive way for builders to help home buyers increase the comfort and energy efficiency of their homes. Typical costs are $40 to $60 per unit, although savings vary substantially depending upon their use. Programmable thermostats work with most types of central HVAC systems, but there are special programmable heat pump thermostats, so do not use conventional models with heat pumps. Like nonprogrammable thermostats, they should be located out of direct sunlight and away from heat-producing appliances, registers, and other sources of heating and cooling. A good spot is 4 to 5 feet above the floor in an interior hallway or near an air return.

Air Conditioning Equipment – Rules of Thumb

👍 Correctly size the unit for its intended application. Save costs by not oversizing. Oversizing results in humidity problems and poor energy performance.

👍 Select units with the ENERGY STAR® label.

👍 Shade outdoor units with trees, shrubs, and other landscaping, while being careful not to block airflow to the unit.

👍 Consider units with a multi-speed compressor and/or blower.

👍 Select quiet operating units.

👍 Consider more efficient geothermal heat pumps to meet both heating and cooling loads.

Heating Equipment – Rules of Thumb

👍 In cold climates, select heating equipment with an AFUE rating of 90% or greater.

👍 Select heat pumps and other equipment with the ENERGY STAR® label.

👍 In moderate and warm climates, consider air-source and geothermal heat pumps for both heating and cooling loads.

👍 Size the heating system appropriately. Save material costs by not oversizing.

👍 Connect the heating system to programmable thermostats.

Additional Resources

A Builder's Guide to Residential HVAC Systems, NAHB Research Center, Home Builder Press. 1997. Provides extensive information about HVAC sizing, design, and equipment selection, and also includes energy-efficiency considerations.

Consumers' Guide to Certified Efficiency Ratings for Residential Heating and Water Heating Equipment, Gas Appliance Manufacturers Association, Arlington, Virginia. This directory lists the efficiency ratings of all models of gas furnaces, boilers, and water heaters according to manufacturer.

A Builder's Guide to Energy Efficient Homes in Georgia, Southface Energy Institute, Inc. Offers excellent descriptions and diagrams of different HVAC systems. Lots of information on sizing, installation, and duct work.

U.S. Department of Energy Office of Building Technology, State and Community Programs offers a comprehensive set of information on all forms of building technology, including HVAC systems. www.eere.energy.gov/buildings

Web Resources

www.ashrae.org
   American Society of Heating, Refrigeration, and Air-Conditioning
   Engineers, Inc.
www.toolbase.org/ToolbaseResources
   Toolbase Services: Heating, Ventilating, and Air Conditioning
www.builtgreen.org/articles/0308_HVAC_sizing.htm
   Built Green Colorado: HVAC Equipment Sizing Calcs

Interactions

See the following sections for information on how Heating and Air
Conditioning Equipment affects other building considerations:

WATER HEATING

Water heating is the second largest energy use in new homes after space conditioning (heating and cooling). The five areas where improvement is possible are:

- More efficient hot water generation
- Reduced storage (or standby) losses in hot water equipment
- Reduced piping losses
- Reduction in hot water temperatures to provide the minimum acceptable temperature for intended use
- Reduced end use.

Water Heater Efficiency

Water heater efficiency is described by the Energy Factor (EF) rating. The EF takes into account the overall efficiency at which the fuel (gas, electricity, or oil) is converted to useful water heating energy, including standby losses.

In all cases, a higher EF indicates a higher efficiency. However, electric water heater EFs should not be compared to gas. Often, the additional cost of a high-efficiency unit is quite low compared to the savings that can be achieved. Higher efficiencies are realized through increased tank insulation and, for gas- and oil-fired heaters, through improved heat transfer from the flame to the water.

Gas-fired water heaters generally cost $150 to $200 more than electric water heaters of similar construction and warranty. Yet gas water heaters typically cost *less* to operate in comparison to electric water heaters. Consider more than just equipment cost when choosing which fuel to use for water heating (Chapter 2, Renewable Energy, "Solar Water Heating Systems"). Local utilities may offer electricity generated by 100% renewable sources.

If a gas water heater is chosen, consider a direct-vented condensing unit or power-vented unit. Condensing units are expensive (usually around $2,000). They have EFs of approximately 0.85, however, and generally have large enough capacity to provide space heating via radiant floors or hydronic coil.

Insulate Hot Water Tank and Lines

Reduce piping and standby losses—losses that can account for more than 30% of water heating energy—by wrapping the storage tank and insulating pipes. Wrap storage tanks with R-16 insulation jackets, being careful not to cover the relief or drain valve or the air inlet to the gas or oil burner. Insulate hot water pipes from the heater to their end use with R-6.

Be sure to insulate all hot water pipes in unconditioned space and the first 6 feet extending out of the water heater. Water jackets and insulation are inexpensive, easy to install, and readily available. Water jackets start at $10. Heat traps and anti-convection valves also reduce heat losses.

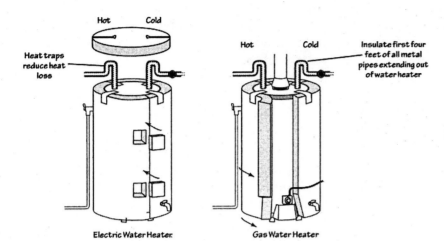

Insulating Jackets for Electric and Gas Water Heaters

Electric Water Heater

Gas Water Heater

Reducing Losses at Remote Fixtures

There are several strategies for reducing water use and water heating losses that occur when hot water is drawn from a fixture that is distant from the water heater:

- Locate the water heater or water storage tank in close proximity to the bathroom, washing machine, and kitchen.
- Consider point-of-use, instantaneous water heating systems.
- Use energy-efficient, on-demand recirculating systems.
- Use a manifold PEX water supply tubing system in which 3/8" diameter "home runs" are run directly from the water heater to the fixtures.

Set Water Heater to 120 Degrees

Set water heater temperature to 120 degrees. Higher temperatures lead to scalding and more standby losses, while lower temperatures can lead to Legionella bacteria in the water tank. If higher temperatures are desired for washing dishes, use dishwashers with booster heaters.

Alternative Water Heating Systems

Consider water heating options such as solar water heating, heat pump water heaters, heat recovery processes, and combination space and water heating systems. These systems and options can significantly improve efficiency over traditional hot water tank systems.

Instantaneous water heaters only heat water as it is called for and do not require significant amounts of storage. This means they have minimal stand-by losses. Point-of-use instantaneous water heaters heat water at each individual end use rather than in a central location.

Water Heating – Rules of Thumb

   👍 Locate the water heater as close as possible to the bathroom, kitchen, and washing machine in order to reduce heat losses.

   👍 Size correctly to meet demand and use the smallest water heater possible. Smaller water heaters are typically more efficient because they have lower standby losses.

   👍 Install heat traps to reduce convective heat loss from the tank.

   👍 Insulate hot water tanks with R-16 jackets without covering the relief or drain valve or the air inlet to the gas or oil burner.

   👍 Insulate hot water pipes from the heater to the end use with R-6 insulation. If this level of insulation is prohibitive, insulate all hot water pipes in unconditioned space and the first 6 feet extending out from the water heater.

   👍 Set water heater temperature to 120 degrees. If higher temperatures are desired for dish washing, select dishwashers with booster heaters.

Additional Resources

Builder's Guide to Energy Efficient Homes, Southface Energy Institute, Inc. September 1999. Good general information. See p. 117 for Heat Recovery Units/Desuperheaters.

The Consumers' Directory of Certified Efficiency Ratings for Heating and Water Heating Equipment, Gas Appliance Manufacturers Association (GAMA). Provides a concise listing of Energy Factors for water heaters of all fuel types. www.gamanet.org

Web Resources

www.eere.energy.gov/buildings/info/homes/choosingwater.html
U.S. Department of Energy, Energy Efficiency and Renewable Energy: Energy Efficient Water Heating

www.toolbase.org/Home-Building-Topics/Energy-Efficiency/energy-efficient-appliances
Toolbase Services: Water Heaters

Interactions

See the following sections for information on how Water Heating affects other building considerations:

LIGHTING

Standard incandescent bulbs are the most common but also the most inefficient lighting sources for homes. The lighting industry has produced a number of alternative lighting systems. When designing a lighting plan, consult with knowledgeable professionals about optimum lighting levels and different types of fixtures and lamps. In addition to the purchase price, consider the long-term energy costs of fixtures before choosing any particular one. Energy-efficient lighting produces less heat, thereby saving money on cooling as well as lighting costs.

Energy-efficient lighting should be placed in areas of high continuous use such as the kitchen, sitting areas, and outside the home. Use task or accent lighting for specific areas where greater illumination is desired, rather than over-illuminating the entire room. Daylight from windows, light pipes, and other glazing should be maximized without incurring an energy penalty of unwanted heat gain or loss. Motion sensors, photo sensors, and timers should be part of the exterior lighting design.

This section discusses the following alternatives to incandescent lighting:

- Daylight
- Compact and other fluorescent lighting for indoor use
- Sealed IC recessed lighting
- Outdoor lighting
- Occupant and photo sensors, dimmers, and other controls

Daylight

Bringing in natural light is the ideal way to increase comfort and aesthetics in a home while reducing energy consumption. Common examples include light tubes or light pipes, skylights, and clerestory windows. Careful consideration should be given to skylights and windows to avoid unwanted heat gains and losses (see Chapter 2, Renewable Energy, "Passive Solar Design"). Light pipes provide natural light for the home's interior or in areas where other issues, such as privacy in a bathroom, restrict the use of traditional glazing. Light pipes can also protect the home from unwanted heat gains and losses associated with traditional windows. Light pipes typically range in cost from $200 to $500. Light tubes and skylights must be well sealed to prevent air infiltration or water leakage.

Compact and Other Fluorescent Lighting for Indoor Use

Fluorescent lighting has improved dramatically. Fluorescent fixtures that use electronic ballasts do not flicker or hum. Select bulbs with a high color rendition index (80 or higher), sometimes referred to as CRI. These emit high-quality light that is close to incandescent lighting. Compact fluorescent bulbs easily fit in recessed, wall, or ceiling mounted fixtures, and many models can be used with dimmers. Fluorescent lights last as much as 10 times longer than incandescent bulbs and reduce energy use by 50% to 70%, although they are more expensive than incandescent bulbs. Compact and other fluorescent bulbs are widely available in a range of wattages and bulb sizes.

Fluorescent Lighting Guidelines

Type of Room	Size of Room	Amount of Light Needed (Watts)
Living Room, Bedroom,	under 150 sf	40–60
Family Room, or	150–250 sf	60–80
Recreation Room	over 250 sf	.33 Watts/sf
Kitchen,	75 sf	55–70
Laundry, or	75–120 sf	60–80
Workshop	over 120 sf	.75 Watts/sf

Recessed Lighting

Fixtures should not penetrate into any insulated area. According to Austin-based architect Peter Pfeiffer, "They tend to let a lot of heat out in the winter and humidity in during the summer, even the so-called airtight ones." They are especially problematic in cathedral ceilings. In cold climates, if they are near the eaves, they leak heat into the attic space and can contribute to ice dams.

Outdoor Lighting

Metal halide and compact fluorescent are the most energy-efficient choices for outdoor lighting. Use motion detectors to control outdoor lighting. Motion detectors cost approximately $30. The detectors will ensure the lights are on for safety and security purposes when needed and off at all other times.

Solar powered lights that charge during the day are a good option for lighting pathways and driveways. They typically cost $30 to $50 per fixture.

Outdoor lighting should be pointed down toward the ground or home exterior to prevent unnecessary nighttime light pollution.

Occupant and Photo Sensors, Dimmers, and Other Controls

Consider using solid-state dimmers and multilevel switches for indoor lighting. Dimmers are a popular lighting control for indoor lights and are compatible with almost all types of lighting, including many fluorescent lamps, such as compact models. Occupancy and photo sensors are primarily used for outdoor lighting, although they can be used inside the home in seldom-used spaces or areas that are daylit or use electric lights.

Energy-Efficient Lighting — Rules of Thumb

👍 Increase the amount of natural light in a home and reduce energy costs.

👍 Consider using light pipes to bring natural light into the interior of homes.

👍 Compact and other fluorescent lighting should be used as much as possible, particularly in the kitchen, sitting areas, and outside.

👍 Select fluorescent fixtures with electronic ballasts to eliminate noise and flicker.

👍 Avoid recessed lighting in insulated ceilings.

👍 Use motion detectors or occupancy sensors to control outdoor lighting.

👍 Use metal halide or fluorescent fixtures for outdoor lighting.

👍 Use solid-state dimmers and multilevel switches that allow for variable lighting levels.

Additional Resources

Illuminating Engineering Society of North America (IESNA) publishes helpful information on lighting products, including controls. www.iesna.org; 800-862-2086

Sustainable Building Technical Manual: Green Building Design, Construction, and Operations, Public Technology, Inc., U.S. Green Building Council, U.S. Department of Energy, and U.S. Environmental Protection Agency. 1996. Chapter 9. PTI, 1301 Pennsylvania Ave. NW, Washington, D.C., 20004-1793. 800-852-4934; pti.nw.dc.us

A Builder's Guide to Energy Efficient Homes in Georgia, Georgia Environmental Facilities Authority, Division of Energy Resources. September 1999. p. 124–125. Southface Energy Institute, Inc., 241 Pine Street, Atlanta, GA 30308. 404-872-3549; www.southface.org

Lighting Research Center. 21 Union Street, Troy, NY 12180-3352. 518-687-7100; www.lrc.rpi.edu

Web Resources

www.eere.energy.gov/buildings/info/homes/buylighting.html
   U.S. Department of Energy, Energy Efficiency and Renewable Energy: Energy Efficient Lighting

www.energystar.gov/index.cfm?c=lighting.pr_lighting
   U.S. Department of Energy, Energy Star: Change a Light, Change the World

www.toolbase.org/ToolbaseResources
   Toolbase Services

www.wbdg.org/design/efficientlighting.php
   Whole Building Design Guide: Energy Efficient Lighting

Interactions

See the following sections for information on how Lighting affects other building considerations:

APPLIANCES

A builder's influence regarding which appliances are purchased for a home varies from complete control to none at all. Regardless of who is procuring them, appliances are often overlooked as a means of improving energy efficiency in homes. Appliances consume nearly one fifth of a home's energy, with the refrigerator commanding a 9% share. Use "Energy-Efficient Appliances – Rules of Thumb" as a checklist for your appliance decisions.

Typical Energy Costs for Appliances			
Appliance	Average Model ($/yr)	High Efficiency Model ($/yr)	10-Year Savings
Refrigerator (manual defrost)	56	36	$200
Refrigerator/freezer (frost free)	96	56	$400
Freezer (frost free)	108	60	$480
Electric range	48	40	$80
Gas range	36	28	$80
Electric clothes dryer	56	44	$120
Gas clothes dryer	24	20	$40
Dishwasher*	56	36	$200
Color television	20	8	$120
Lighting	60	28	$320

* Includes cost of water heating. Source: Adapted from "Saving Energy and Money with Home Appliances," by the Massachusetts Audubon Society and the American Council for an Energy-Efficient Economy

Buy ENERGY STAR® Appliances

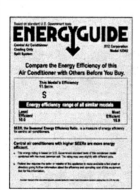

Money Isn't All You're Saving

In general, builders should select cost-effective, energy-efficient models with the ENERGY STAR® label. ENERGY STAR® is a government-sponsored program that identifies products that are significantly more energy efficient than the minimum government standards. The amount by which an appliance must exceed the minimum standards varies for each type of product. ENERGY STAR® labels can be found on almost all major appliances. Selecting products with the ENERGY STAR® label can be an effective and easy way to market your home as a cost-effective and energy-efficient house.

When buying ENERGY STAR® appliances is not possible, builders should select appliances that are rated among the more efficient in their class by the yellow EnergyGuide label. At this time, EnergyGuide labels are not required on all types of appliances. These labels compare how much it will cost to operate one appliance per year, in comparison to competing models with the highest and lowest annual energy costs. Check with your state energy office as well as your utility company to see if there are incentives or rebate programs that support installation of energy-efficient appliances in your homes.

Refrigerators/Freezers

Refrigerators/freezers are big energy users because they operate 24 hours a day, 365 days a year. Efficient models can cost half as much to operate as inefficient ones. ENERGY STAR® refrigerators are at least 10% more efficient than the minimum standards effective as of July 2001. In general, most of the energy-efficient models are in the 16 to 20 cubic foot range. Side-by-side refrigerators, automatic ice dispensers, and through-the-door water dispensers are popular options that, unfortunately, decrease a model's efficiency and therefore increase operating costs. When designing the kitchen, locate the refrigerator away from heat sources such as ovens, ranges, dishwashers, forced air vents or radiators, and direct sunlight. Also be sure to provide adequate ventilation around the refrigerator. Without adequate ventilation, the compressor works harder because the heat expelled by the coils cannot escape.

Dishwashers

Water heating accounts for 80% of the energy consumed by a dishwasher. In general, models that use less water use less energy. As of January 2001, ENERGY STAR® dishwasher models use at least 25% less energy than is called for by government standards (the old specification was 13%). Builders should select models that include the following characteristics:

- An Energy Factor of 0.58 or higher
- Light, medium, and heavy wash settings
- Energy saving "no-heat dry" or "air-dry" switch
- Booster or supplemental water heater that allows the water heater to be set to 120 degrees

Dishwashers range in price from $300 to $1,000. Builders may market energy- and water-efficient dishwashers from several additional perspectives, including quiet operation, performance, ease of use, and reliability.

Dishwasher Cost-Effectiveness Example

Performance	Base Model[a]	Recommended Level
Energy Factor	0.46	0.58
Annual Energy Use	700 kWh	555 kWh
With Electric Water Heating		
Annual Energy Cost	$42	$33
Lifetime Energy Cost	$400	$320
Lifetime Energy Savings	–	$80
With Gas Water Heating		
Annual Energy Cost	$21	$16
Lifetime Energy Cost	$220	$170
Lifetime Energy Savings	–	$50

[a] The efficiency (Energy Factor) of the Base Model is just sufficient to meet current U.S. DOE national appliance standards.

Ovens, Stoves, and Ranges

Convection ovens are 33% more efficient than standard ovens. Gas ovens and stoves are typically less expensive to operate but are more expensive to purchase. Electronic cooktops with ceramic glass covers are more efficient than coil or disk electric stoves. Induction elements that use electromagnetic energy to heat the pan are the most efficient.

Clothes Washers

Water heating can account for 90% of a clothes washer's energy use. ENERGY STAR® washers, which come in top-loading and front-loading models, use 30% to 40% less energy than conventional washers. Front-loading models, which are also called tumble washers or horizontal axis machines, typically get clothes cleaner and are gentler on clothes than traditional top loading machines. They are the most energy-efficient models, with average energy savings of 60%, although more efficient, advanced-design top-loaders are available. Front-loading machines also use 36% less water than traditional washers, and some spin clothes faster, which dries clothes better and reduces time in the drier. Depending on the amount and manner of use, as well as water, electricity, and gas rates, front-loading machines can save consumers $100 or more during each year of the machine's 13-15 year lifespan. These savings far exceed the $200 to $300 additional purchase cost. Builders should select washers that offer several wash and rinse cycle (temperature) options as well as several sizes of loads. Front loaders also tend to be more reliable, because they do not have an agitator (the part that most often fails on washers).

Clothes Dryers

Like most appliances, clothes dryers can be gas or electric. Where natural gas is available, gas dryers have historically been less expensive to operate but have a higher first cost. Electric dryers are just the opposite: more expensive to operate with a lower first cost. Builders should select models that detect "dryness" and then shut off automatically, or those that offer energy-saving settings. Some dryers have moisture sensors that typically save from 10% to 15% over standard dryers. Over time, these models save a considerable amount of energy.

Energy-Efficient Appliances — Rules of Thumb

👍 Buy and install ENERGY STAR® rated appliances. Alternatively, select appliances that are rated among the most efficient in their class as indicated on the EnergyGuide label.

👍 Allow for adequate ventilation areas around the refrigerator.

👍 Electronic cooktops with ceramic glass covers are more efficient than disk or coil stoves.

👍 Use quietness, performance, and other non-energy factors to support your selection of energy-efficient dishwashers and clothes washers.

👍 Some front-loading clothes washers also help dry clothes better than top-loading models, allowing for energy savings during the dry cycle.

👍 Consider clothes dryers with moisture and temperature sensors.

👍 Gas appliances are typically less expensive to operate but have a higher first cost.

👍 Check with your local utility and state energy office for rebates and other incentives that may be awarded for installing energy-efficient appliances.

Additional Resources

Consumers Union publishes *Consumer Reports* magazine and the *Consumer Reports Annual Buying Guide,* which rate appliances for reliability, convenience, and efficiency. 800-500-9760; www.consumerreports.org

Home Energy magazine provides energy conservation tips as well as an archive of energy consumption data of old refrigerators. 510-524-5405; www.homeenergy.org/

American Council for an Energy-Efficient Economy (ACEEE) publishes the *Consumer Guide to Home Energy Savings.* 202-429-0063; www.aceee.org

Consortium for Energy Efficiency (CEE) provides information on energy-efficient clothes washers. 617-589-3949; www.cee1.org

DOE and EPA have appliance model listing as part of their ENERGY STAR® program. 800-363-3732; www.energystar.gov

E Source Technology Atlas Series Volume 5 Residential Appliances provides information on appliance specifications and efficiency standards. 720-548-5000; www.esource.com/public/products/prosp_atlas.asp

Web Resources

www.toolbase.org/ToolbaseResources/
   Toolbase Services: Appliances
www.aceee.org/consumerguide/
   American Council for an Energy-Efficient Economy: The Importance of Energy-Efficient Appliances
www.eere.energy.gov/consumer/your_home/appliances/
   U.S. Department of Energy: Appliances
www.energystar.gov/index.cfm?c=appliances.pr_appliances
   ENERGY STAR: Appliances

Interactions

See the following sections for information on how Appliances affect other building considerations:

Chapter 5 Efficient Water Use

INDOOR WATER USE

Since 1900, per capita water use in the United States has quadrupled. Americans now consume an average of over 100 gallons per person per day for indoor and outdoor uses. For homes on public water and sewage systems, water efficiency can be an important community issue. Just about every gallon of water that your local government purifies to meet consumption needs must also be treated after it is used. In this way, two environmental issues, protecting the supply of fresh water and the treatment of wastewater, can be solved through water efficiency.

The table below presents average indoor water consumption data for an American home. The American Water Works Association estimates that indoor water consumption can be reduced by 35% to a total of 45.2 gallons per person per day by installing readily available water-efficient fixtures and appliances and by minimizing leaks.

According to Sandia National Laboratory's estimate, 80% of the cost of delivering water can be directly attributed to energy requirements for pumping, processing, or treating the water. Considering the average cost of domestic water in the U.S. is about $2.50/1000 gallons, the total energy cost associated with providing residential water in our country is $20 billion per year. That's about 3% of our country's $700 billion energy bill. To solve this problem in the short term, conservation of water must become a top priority in this country. With 97% of the world's water in our oceans and only three-tenths of one percent of the world's water being potable, our next goal must be to focus on non-polluting, desalination strategies . . . derived from solar energy.

—Mike Nicklas, "Chair's Corner,"
Solar Today, Sept/Oct 2003

Typical Indoor Household Water Use		
Type of Use	Daily Use (gallons per person)	Approximate % of Total Indoor Use
Toilets	18.5	26.7
Clothes Washers	15.0	21.7
Showers	11.6	16.8
Faucets	10.9	15.7
Leaks	9.5	13.7
Other	1.6	2.2
Baths	1.2	1.7
Dishwashers	1.0	1.4
Total	**69.3**	**100.0**

Source: American Water Works Association 2006 (www.drinktap.org)

Note: This table does not include residential water use *outside* the home, which brings the typical total to about 105 gallons per person per day. Typical residential water consumption for lawns, gardens, and car washing is highly variable across the country, ranging between 25 and 200 gallons per person per day.

Low-Flow Toilets

Federal law (Energy Policy Act of 1992) requires 1.6 gallons per flush (gpf) toilets for all new construction. Because quality can vary greatly, it is important to research and carefully select toilets, showerheads, and faucets. Some of the first low-flow toilets did not perform adequately. Recently, manufacturers have produced much-improved low-flow toilets that work well and are affordable. Builders may also want to consider using dual-flush low-flow toilets and composting toilets where codes permit.

Low-Flow Faucets

The Energy Policy Act of 1992 limits faucet and showerhead water use to 2.5 gallons per minute (gpm) at 80 psi. Builders should specify faucets with a 2.2 gpm rating or less. Aerators placed on faucets add air to the water stream, thus boosting the effectiveness of the flow and reducing water consumption. Flow-restrictors are not recommended in areas with low water pressure.

Low-Flow Showerheads

Superior-performing low-flow showerheads with flow rates between 1.5 and 2.0 gpm are available. Homeowner complaints regarding low-flow showerheads are most often associated with their "feel" and eventual clogging. Be wary of atomizer and aerator showerheads that deliver water in fine droplets to save water. (Aerators are recommended for faucets but not for showerheads; the cooling effect is so great with these types of heads that users feel their shower is of poor quality.) Avoid flow-restrictor showerheads in areas with low water pressure. Instead, look for showerheads with flow rates less than 2.5 gpm that have the feel of higher flow and are guaranteed against clogging. These are commonly available at an added cost of approximately $10 per head. Not all showerheads have the same flow rate; research the available brands and models and select carefully. Some showerheads also use temporary cut-off valves that attach to or are incorporated into the showerhead. They stop the water flow when the individual is soaping or shampooing. When the water flow is reactivated, it emerges at the same temperature, eliminating the need to remix the hot and cold water.

Appliances and Recirculating Systems

See "Appliances" in Chapter 4, Energy Efficiency, for information on dishwashers and clothes washers. Some builders may also wish to consider hot water recirculating systems. These systems are best employed in homes with faucets distant from the hot water heater. Several types are available for as little as $350. Water savings are achieved when homeowners no longer run a faucet for minutes before hot water arrives. Energy savings are also realized.

Leaks

Leaks are insidious and costly, averaging 10% of a home's water consumption. Prevention is the key. Use quality pipes, fittings, valves, and other hardware (see "Plumbing Hardware/NSF Cerfitication" below). In addition, carefully inspect the work of plumbing subcontractors. Once the plumbing system is complete, the American Water Works Association suggests an easy "zero-read" test to check for leaks. Check the water meter during a period when no water is being used. Do this by reading the last two right hand digits or dials. Wait 30 minutes (the longer the better as some leaks are cyclical) and then take another reading. If usage has occurred, first check the flapper valve and overflow level in all toilets. If no problems are detected there, pipelines or an in-ground irrigation system may be likely sources of the leak(s). Be sure to pass on the zero-read test to your home buyers so they can continue to check for leaks on an annual basis.

Plumbing Hardware / NSF Certification

NSF International, The Public Health and Safety Company™, is a nonprofit, nongovernmental organization. NSF International is a leader in standards development, product certification, education, and risk management for public health and safety.

Select NSF-approved plumbing fixtures and fittings that are of top quality in terms of water conservation and leak resistance. Obtain proof of NSF certification for each plumbing component. The NSF mark on plastic plumbing products and materials confirms that NSF has assessed and certified a product's conformity with NSF Standard 14 requirements for its intended end use. Plastic piping products designed for potable water applications must also meet the health effects requirements of ANSI/NSF 61, which ensure that any impurities imparted indirectly from a product into the drinking water are within acceptable levels.

Potable Water Quality

To ensure adequate water quality, upon completion of the plumbing system, flush the system and conduct water sampling at taps and service lines entering the home. At a minimum, test for lead, copper, pH, arsenic, and turbidity. Water quality results should be within EPA maximum contaminant levels and action levels (EPA 40 Code of Federal Regulations, Parts 141-149). To achieve the highest quality water for cooking and drinking, consider installing filters at taps and/or at the service line(s) or house main. Some filter systems may require periodic filter replacement, addition of chemicals, and, owing to back wash requirements, increased water use.

Efficient Interior Water Use – Rules of Thumb

👍 Low-flow toilets may significantly reduce the total number of gallons used in a typical home. Some models perform significantly better than others; research and carefully select 1.6 gpf toilets.

👍 Install low-flow, non-clogging showerheads (1.5 to 2.0 gpm) and faucets (less than 2.2 gpm).

👍 Minimize leaks by educating home buyers about plumbing maintenance (this also prevents call-backs and owner dissatisfaction). Use the zero-read method to test for leaks.

👍 Ensure plumbing integrity during construction by inspection and by using NSF-certified components that meet ANSI/NSF 61 and NSF Standard 14.

👍 Flush newly installed plumbing systems and conduct water samplings at service lines.

Additional Resources

Vickers, Amy, *Handbook of Water Use and Conservation*, Lewis Publishers/CRS Press. 1999.

"An Energy-Saving Product That's Actually Convenient?" *Energy Design Update*. July 1997, p. 8. This article reviews one hot water recirculating system.

The Water Smart Home Program, Greater Atlanta Home Builders Association. This program is a well-designed and comprehensive water conservation program developed in partnership by the Atlanta HBA and the Georgia Water Wise Council.

"Dishing Out Dollars,"*Consumer Reports*. March 1998, p.37.
A comprehensive review of energy- and water-efficient dishwashers. www.consumerreports.org

The Resource Guide to Sustainable Landscapes and Gardens, Environmental Resources, Inc., Salt Lake City, Utah. Lists over 1,100 environmentally responsible landscaping materials.

Guide to Resource Efficient Building Elements, 6th Edition, Center for Resourceful Building Technology. Contains a section specifically devoted to landscaping materials; includes supplier lists.

Web Resources

www.epa.gov/owm/water-efficiency/pp/plumbing/het.htm
U.S. EPA: Low Flow Toilets
www.conserveh2o.org/fixtures.html
Regional Water Providers Consortium: Water Saving Fixtures
www.nsf.org/business/plumbing_system_components/
NSF International, The Public Health and Safety Company: Water
www.toolbase.org
Toolbase Services

Interactions

See the following sections for information on how Indoor Water Use affects other building considerations:

OUTDOOR WATER USE

Depending on location, residential water consumption for outdoor use can range between 25 and 200 gallons per day per house, accounting for an average of 50% to 77% of a household's seasonal water use.

Currently, the price paid for water does not necessarily reflect either the costs of purification and treatment or supply and demand. Eastern and midwestern states are depleting their aquifers faster than they are being replenished. A growing number of western states are importers of fresh water. Both trends mean that many communities will continue to spend more money to supply wasteful water habits than they do now. This will require a major expansion of existing infrastructure at an expense of at least several hundred million dollars per state. Home builders can be part of the solution by designing and building homes with lawns, landscaping, irrigation, and drainage plans that use water more efficiently. Using treated water for these purposes puts unnecessary pressure on both natural and municipal resources.

Xeriscaping With Native and Drought-Resistant Plants

Xeriscaping landscape designs concentrate on water conservation by using native plants and avoiding imported species that are not suited to the local climate. They are more likely to survive once the homeowner moves in and require less maintenance, nutrients, fertilizers, and especially, water than many exotic (non-native) species. Plants that are not native but are from areas similar in climate, rainfall, and soil type are preferable to exotic species, providing they are not invasive.

Xeriscaping and Landscaping Planting Plans

Consider xeriscaping and landscape planning early in the design and construction phases of a home. Designing xeriscapes requires 1) knowledge of the plant materials in the site's hardiness zone, 2) knowledge of the interrelationships between plant materials and the environment, 3) an understanding of soil and soil moisture requirements of each plant, 4) understanding of horticulture, and 5) design ability so that the plants fulfill both aesthetic and functional requirements. In many cases, the builder is not involved in the planting portion of the project at all. However, there are several advantages to considering the location and type of plants, grasses, and trees early in the design phase of the project:

- Topsoil can be placed strategically, drainage patterns created, and contours shaped during the backfill and grading phases.
- Adequate holes for planting trees can be dug while a backhoe is on site.

- Provision for landscaping costs can be made early in the project and included in the budget.
- The type and location of the irrigation system can more closely fit the requirements of the vegetation.

A landscape architect can provide useful information about soil type, plant varieties, and light, nutrient, water, and planting requirements. Consult your local nursery, soil or water conservation department, agriculture extension office or university, department of parks, or mail-order nursery and seed companies. All are good sources of information. Information regarding specific plant varieties is also available through local nurseries, soil and water conservation departments, and numerous published sources, as well as through landscape architects.

Minimizing Use of Lawn Turf by Using Native Grasses

Select native grasses (or even buffalo grass or fescue), shrubs, wildflowers, and other groundcovers in lieu of traditional grasses such as Kentucky blue-grass and rye. Native plants can use as little as one fifth the amount of water as their "imported" counterparts. Native species are a water-efficient and attractive way to reduce lawn maintenance and pollution. A traditional well-manicured lawn may require up to 10 pounds of pesticides and fertilizers per acre per year. A two-cycle, gas-powered lawn mower creates as much pollution in 30 minutes as a car driven 172 miles. Replacing resource-intensive turf grasses with native plants, grasses, and wildflowers also aids in the restoration of wildlife and other plants that may be threatened.

The selection of seed or sod is based on a variety of factors: cost, appearance, maintenance requirements, availability, and water requirements. There are no set relationships among these factors; drought-tolerant or lower water-need turf grasses are not necessarily more or less expensive than other grass varieties.

Pervious Materials

Using pervious materials for patios, paths, and driveways allows for natural drainage and enables water to be reabsorbed into the soil, thereby reducing stormwater run-off. Among suitable materials and methods are stone dust, gravel, crushed stone, brick, masonry, grid pavers, pervious concrete pavers, grid-stabilized grass, and combinations of clay and sand as a hard base. Paving stones or brick laid in a pervious material will also allow for more uniform drainage than those set in mortar. Over time, some of these materials will lose their pervious qualities after compaction from use.

Typically, sand, gravel, and crushed stone will be relatively inexpensive. Be sure to border these areas to keep the materials in place. Home buyers should decide whether they prefer loose or hard surfaces for footpaths and driveways.

For homeowners choosing to build their own decks or patios, patios may be a greener option than decks made from CCA (chromated copper arsenate) pressure-treated lumber, which has been phased out by the EPA. Manufacturers cannot use CCA chemicals after December 31, 2003, but this product may still be found in lumber yards. Homeowners should obtain information about more environmentally benign building materials that are suitable for outdoor use. See Chapter 7, Materials, for further information about porch and patio materials.

Irrigation Technology: Timers, Sensors, and Other Controls

Despite perceptions, studies have shown that automated, in-ground sprinkler systems typically use 20% to 30% more water than manual hosing. This is mainly due to overwatering and leaks. Homeowners who insist on a sprinkler system should consider a drip system (see below). Otherwise, they should install programmable switches, timers, or rain sensors to improve the efficiency of the delivery system. Automated irrigation systems that are not responsive to daily watering conditions actually result in an even higher average water use. Separate timers for watering systems run between $30 and $50. Irrigation controllers cost about $40 for the mechanical type and $100 to $150 for digital models.

Drip Irrigation

Drip irrigation systems are the most efficient watering methods available, provided that leaks are minimized. Conventional sprinkler systems lose 30% to 70% of total water to evaporation and runoff. Drip irrigation systems can be on the surface or buried. Surface systems can be installed after home completion by the owner, whereas subsurface systems are completed as part of contractor's landscaping plan. The reduced flow rate and elimination of airborne water delivery makes these systems significantly more efficient. However, their efficiency is dependent on proper installation and elimination of leaks. Another advantage of drip irrigation systems is the lowered potential for leaf mold and mildew growth and weeds because the water is targeted at the root zone of the desirable vegetation. Measures may need to be taken to control root invasion into the drip piping. Drip irrigation systems are not appropriate for lawn areas.

Depending on soil type and the number of emitters, the materials for a drip irrigation system will cost approximately $250 per 1,000 linear feet. Materials are readily available from plumbing suppliers.

Wastewater Treatment and Reclaimed Water

Reclaimed water is one of several forms of water reuse. Specifically, it can be water from a wastewater treatment plant (WWTP) that is diverted into another use, such as landscape irrigation. In some areas of the United States, reclaimed water may be referred to as irrigation quality or "IQ" water. The use of wastewater for nonpotable uses can greatly reduce the demand on potable water sources, and its use is encouraged by many organizations, including FEMP, EPA, and the American Water Works Association.

For a reclaimed water project to be successful, one or more of the following conditions must be present:

- The community lacks an affordable water supply or a high-quality freshwater supply.
- Local public policy encourages or mandates water conservation.
- High-quality effluent is available from a WWTP.
- Reuse is the most cost-effective means of wastewater effluent disposal.

The quality of the reclaimed water must be reviewed to ensure that there will be no adverse effects from long-term use, such as landscape damage due to salt buildup. Note that the use of reclaimed water may be restricted by code.

Rain Catchment

Where codes permit, collected rain water can be used for toilet flushing and landscape and garden irrigation. For watering purposes, a rain catchment or water recovery system can be as simple as roof gutters with downspouts directed into catchment barrels. Rainwater recovery systems attached to some type of distribution system will likely require a pump, and therefore, a filtration system to protect the pump and delivery system. Simple rain barrel systems that connect directly to gutters and have a garden hose outlet range from approximately $100 to $200. All but the simplest rainwater recovery systems are difficult to install as retrofits. Rain catchment systems reduce a homeowner's treated water consumption and reduce stress on local combined sewer systems.

Water Harvesting
In this illustration, rainwater ❶ is collected in a cistern ❷, for controlled release over time ❸.
Illustration: Bruce Hendler

Greywater

Where codes permit, a significant amount of potable water can be readily reused for various nonpotable purposes. Greywater is water from uses such as showers and bathroom sinks that contains a minimum amount of contamination and, with minimal processing, can be used again for non-potable applications such as toilet flushing and non-edible landscape irrigation. Greywater may contain pathogens, and must be treated prior to any reuse. Humans should avoid contact with greywater before treatment. Installation of greywater systems is best done during construction, as retrofits can be difficult.

Case Study: Wastewater Treatment

Although water prices vary greatly around the country, reclaimed water costs significantly less than potable water. For example, in Jupiter, Florida, the price of potable water is now $0.37/1000 liters ($1.70/1000 gallons), versus $0.06/1000 liters ($0.26/1000 gallons) for reclaimed water. Similar pricing differences occur wherever reclaimed water is available.

Efficient Exterior Water Use – Rules of Thumb

👍 Xeriscaping rather than typical high water-use landscaping can reduce lawn maintenance, water consumption, and air pollution. Select native trees, plants, and bushes that are drought resistant, suited to your local climate, and capable of contributing to the energy efficiency of a home by shading it from the summer sun and blocking winter winds.

👍 Select drought-resistant native grasses or other ground covers in lieu of traditional lawn grasses to reduce lawn maintenance and limit water consumption.

👍 Select pervious surfaces for driveways and pathways.

👍 Consider installing a rain catchment system to offset outdoor water use.

👍 Consider installing a greywater system to offset outdoor water use.

Additional Resources

Atienze, J., and J. Craytor, "Plumbing Efficiency through Grey-Water Recycling," *Consulting Specifying Engineer.* March 1995, p. 58.

Farrugia, S., "The Three Rs of Water Conservation," *Consulting Specifying Engineer.* October 1994, p. 18.

Group Raindrops 1995, *Rainwater and You: 100 Ways to Use Rainwater*, Organizing Committee for the Tokyo International Rainwater Utilization Conferences. Sumida City Office Building, 1-23-20 Asumabashi, Sumida City, Tokyo 130, Japan. 1995.

Hightshoe, Gary L.; and Harlen D. Groe, "North American Plant File." Classifies the environmental suitability, aesthetic qualities, cultural requirements, and design uses for 3,600 plants.

Lehr, Valentine A., *"Grey Water Systems,"* Heating/Piping/Air Conditioning. January 1987, p. 103-113.

Rosenbaum, Marc, "Converting 'Waste' into Nutrients—Treating Household Organic Waste." An *Environmental Building News* article on composting toilets. www.buildinggreen.com/features/mr/waste.html

NSF, International Standard 41: *Wastewater Recycled/Reuse and Water Conservation Devices.* www.nsf.org

Rocky Mountain Institute, Water Efficiency; *A Resource Guide for Utility Managers, Community Planners, and Other Decisionmakers*, U.S. EPA Office of Water/Office of Wastewater. 1991.

Water Conservation Plan Guidelines, U.S. Environmental Protection Agency, Office of Water. 1998. EPA-832-D-98-001

Building Greener Building Better, The National Association of Home Builders and the NAHB Research Center, Washington, D.C. 2002.

Web Resources

www.plumbingworld.com
This company offers plumbing materials and supplies of all kinds for both inside and outside the home. Great for hard-to-find parts and supplies; also offers a line of drip irrigation materials.

www.floridaplants.com
Although oriented to Florida, this site offers numerous books on all topics from drought-tolerant plants and grasses to landscape design to pest management. In addition to printed publications, there is good information about specific trees, plants, and grasses; soil, water, and light conditions; and disease control. A useful site whether or not you live in Florida.

www.rurdev.usda.gov/rbs/coops/
The U.S. Department of Agriculture's listing of all the state cooperative/ agriculture extension offices, most of which provide useful information about all types vegetation that is particularly well-suited to climates within your state. Information regarding drip irrigation, organic fertilizers and pest control, and other topics pertinent to reducing water use for

the lawn and garden is also available.

www.waterwiser.org

This site is a good jumping off point for accessing information on all aspects of water conservation. Sites pertaining to water conserving appliances, drip irrigation, xeriscaping, landscaping, and community water conservation programs are listed by category.

http://water.usgs.gov

The U.S. Geological Survey provides extensive information and data regarding state and regional water use and water quality. In addition to numerous fact sheets, information about the condition of local streams and waterways is also available.

www.terrylove.com/crtoilet.htm

A Web site that reviews many of the currently available water closets (toilets).

ww.cement.org/buildings/sustainable_green.asp

The Portland Cement Association provides information on concrete pavers and stained/stamped concrete.

www.gcpa.org

The Georgia Concrete and Products Association provides information on pervious concrete and other concrete products.

www.toolbase.org/PDF/TechSets/techset1.pdf

Toolbase Services

Interactions

See the following sections for information on how Outdoor Water Use affects other building considerations:

Chapter 6   Indoor Environmental Quality

Indoor environmental quality (IEQ) refers to the physical quality of the indoor environment as opposed to its aesthetic quality. A major part of IEQ is indoor air quality (IAQ), but IEQ goes beyond air quality to include acoustics and lighting. The major aspects of IEQ include:

- Indoor air quality (levels of pollutants such as building product emissions, external pollutants, dust, and pollen)
- Humidity (moisture in air)
- Air movement (fresh air and drafts)
- Acoustics (noise transmission between rooms)
- Light intensity and quality (from windows, skylights, and artificial lighting)

Indoor Air Quality

There are four principal ways, in order of priority, to promote acceptable indoor air quality:

1. **Eliminate the source.** This is the method of choice that should be used whenever possible. In a tight home, combustion appliances can "backdraft," meaning gases do not go up the flue or out the vent but are discharged into the home. In exceedingly rare cases a significant amount of flue gas can be discharged into the air. Pressure imbalances, often caused by improper air distribution in the air conditioning system, can create this backdrafting.

   Unvented combustion appliances used for space heating, such as "ventless" fireplaces or unvented kerosene heaters, should never be used in green construction because they generate unwanted pollutants and can create large amounts of indoor humidity.

   Pressure differences can also induce air to flow into the living space from a garage. Cars, lawn mowers, and appliances in an attached garage can generate exhaust, which gets carried into the home. Garages should be separated from the rest of the house with a suitable air barrier material, such as gypsum wallboard, housewrap or concrete, with all joints sealed. Special techniques may be needed to prevent radon ("soil gas") from being drawn into the home where site geology presents this problem.

   Use of low-emitting building materials (caulks, sealants, adhesives, particleboard, medium-density fiberboard, and floor coverings, which may emit volatile organic compounds [VOCs]) can reduce some of the pollutant sources commonly found in new homes, such as paints, stains, finishes, carpeting, and flooring. Green materials are covered in the next chapter. Proper storage of toxic chemicals in sealed containers or outside the living space minimizes this source of irritants.

2. **Ventilate close to the source.** Where polluting or moisture-laden sources must mix with room air, as with gas ranges and bathroom showers, the undesirable air should be exhausted as close as possible to the source. It is essential for bath fans and range hoods to operate properly and exhaust to the outdoors. Also, educating occupants to minimize operation of motor vehicles in the garage and ventilating the garage can reduce the build-up of carbon monoxide and other combustion by-products.

3. **Ventilate.** All houses need air exchange to remove stale inside air and excessive moisture. Recently, there has been significant controversy over how much ventilation is needed to maintain good indoor air quality. Most experts agree that the solution is not to build a leaky house that relies on infiltration for air exchange, although some air infiltration will always occur. Accidental leaks may create drafts and discomfort. Appropriate levels of air exchange for residents can be provided in a number of ways, but every home should have some type of controlled, mechanical whole-house ventilation system. ASHRAE 62.2 provides guidance on appropriate ventilation airflow rates, which are generally 7.5 CFM per person plus 1 CFM per 100 SF of living space.

4. **Filter.** If the home has an air distribution system, the conventional filter at the fan can be supplemented with specialized filters, discussed in this chapter. If outside air is brought in by a fan as part of a ventilating strategy, it can be filtered as it enters, reducing the intake of pollen and other outdoor irritants. See the "Filtration Techniques" section later in this chapter.

Preventing Pollution From Attached Garages

Attached garages can be sources of indoor air pollutants in homes, especially in rooms that are adjacent to the garage. Combustion by-products from vehicles and lawn equipment pose a danger to home occupants. In homes with attached garages, auto exhaust has been identified as one of the more significant potential sources of indoor pollutants. Stored paints, solvents, and other household chemicals also emit air pollutants. Whenever possible, do not attach the garage directly. Separate the garage from the home entirely, or connect it with a short, covered walkway, garden landscaping area, an enclosed vestibule, or a laundry, mudroom, or workshop.

Attached garages should be separated from the rest of the house with suitable air barrier material. All joints and openings should be sealed with weatherstripping, caulk, and sealants. Also, occupants should be educated to minimize operation of motor vehicles in the garage and about the proper storage of paints, solvents, chemicals, and other potential sources of pollutants.

Another alternative is to install a garage exhaust fan. These are usually on a timer or connected to the garage door opener to help reduce auto exhaust fumes from entering the living areas of the home. The installed cost is generally less than $200.

Radon Control Measures

The U.S. Environmental Protection Agency (EPA) has developed maps that indicate areas with the highest radon potential. The EPA recommends that homes built in areas with high concentrations of radon (areas designated as Zone 1) be built with radon-resistant features. If you elect not to install a radon venting system, consider roughing-in the needed gas-permeable layer of coarse aggregate beneath the slab, and a polyethylene barrier between the aggregate and slab, for future radon venting. Until a house is completed, it is difficult to predict actual radon levels indoors.

Passive radon venting of a slab consists of running a vertical 3" plastic pipe vent from the foundation to the roof through an interior wall. A gas-permeable layer of coarse aggregate should be placed beneath the slab, and a continuous 6-mil polyethylene barrier between the aggregate and slab. The pipe should be stubbed in with a perforated 'T' fitting at the bottom. Pour slab and seal slab joints with caulk. Active venting uses the same system and installation process with an in-line fan installed in the attic to keep a negative pressure in the area beneath the slab. In new homes, passive systems range from $50 to $300. Installing a fan to convert a passive system to an active system typically costs an additional $200. Installing these systems as retrofits in homes without rough-ins can cost three to six times as much.

Radon Resistant Construction

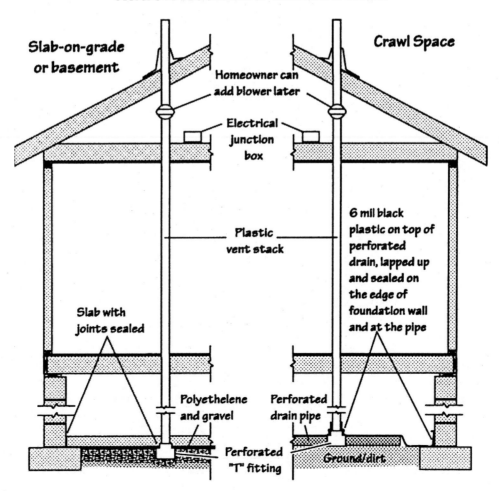

Sample Ventilation Plans

Design 1: Upgraded Spot Ventilation

This relatively simple and inexpensive whole house ventilation system integrates spot ventilation using bathroom and kitchen exhaust fans with an upgraded exhaust fan (usually 100 to 150 cfm) in a centrally located bathroom. When the fan operates, outside air is drawn through leaks in the building enclosure. The fan is controlled by a timer set to provide ventilation at regular intervals. Interior doors are undercut to allow air flow to the central exhaust fan. The fan must be a long-life, high-quality unit that operates quietly. In addition to the automatic ventilation provided by this system, occupants can turn on all exhaust fans manually as needed. Dedicated "outdoor air inlets" often become leaky outlets in 2-story homes and are only needed in small, tight homes.

Design 2: Whole House Ventilation System

This whole house ventilation system uses a centralized two-speed exhaust fan to draw air from the kitchen, bath, laundry, and living area. The blower is controlled by a timer. The system should provide approximately 0.35 ach on low speed and 1.0 ach on high speed, though lower rates are acceptable for larger homes.

Design 3: Heat Recovery Ventilation (HRV) System

An air-to-air heat exchanger draws fresh air outside through a duct into the heat exchange equipment and recaptures heating or cooling energy from stale room air as it is being exhausted. Fresh air flows into the house via a separate duct system, which should be sealed as tightly as the HVAC ductwork. Room air can either be ducted to the exchanger from several rooms or a single source. Some HRV units can be wall-mounted in the living area, while others are designed for utility rooms or basements.

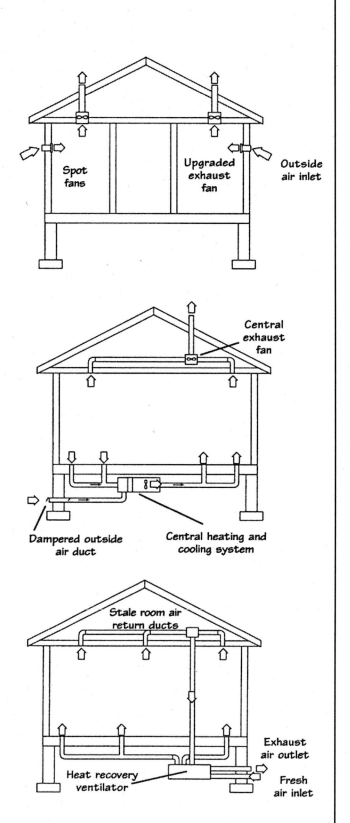

Filtration Techniques

Dust, mold spores, pollen, and wood and tobacco smoke can be reduced with an air filtration system. Homes with central forced-air heating and cooling systems have standard furnace filters that protect the air handler's fan motor and keep dust from the heating and cooling coil. They do little to improve air quality. There are four alternative types of residential air filtration systems: electrostatic, electronic, medium-efficiency (including pleated or extended-surface), and high-efficiency particulate air (HEPA).

Pleated filters are inexpensive, can capture mold and pollen, and last twice as long as standard filters. Look for filters with a MERV rating of at least 8, with larger numbers being more effective at removing small particles that affect respiratory health. These filters will cost more (typically $8 - $12) than a standard filter, but the standard filters only protect the equipment from damage. Less expensive reusable/washable electrostatic filters are not recommended. HEPA filters are available for new construction and as retrofits at a cost of up to $500, with replacement filters costing around $50. With any high efficiency air filter, be sure to account for the pressure drop across the filter in the design of the duct system.

Combustion Safety

Any device relying solely on natural draft can backdraft, resulting in the release of exhaust gas back into the living space. This occurs when negative pressure is created by a fireplace, exhaust fan, or pressure imbalance (from undersized return air ducts, leaky supply ducts in attics, or door closure in homes with central returns). While backdrafting at significant levels is rare, preventative measures should be considered, including powering the exhaust with a fan, providing the appliance with its own supply of combustion air, and specifying a sealed combustion appliance with a separate supply and exhaust.

Controlling Indoor Humidity

Ventilation and indoor moisture control strategies are key to safeguarding the quality of indoor air. A home that is neither too dry nor too humid is preferable. When relative humidity drops below 25%, dry skin, nose, throat, and eyes can result. Most tightly built new homes have enough water-generating activities to make dry conditions relatively rare, but humidification may be necessary in dry climates. Relative humidity above 50% while heating or air conditioning can promote damp conditions, and excessive mechanical ventilation in humid climates can load homes with moisture and cause mold growth and structural deterioration.

Build Vented Storage Space for Toxic Materials

Build a storage area outside the living space for chemical and tool storage. Here you can isolate volatile finishing materials, cleaning agents, and petroleum products, thereby eliminating these agents' capacity to degrade the air quality. The added cost of this type of storage area is likely to be modest. Home buyers with children will likely respond positively to the builder's concern for safety. However, it is important home buyers are made aware that if the outside storage area is expected to experience hot or cold temperatures, they must follow all product storage recommendations.

Range Hoods Ducted to the Outside

Kitchen range hood fans vented to the outdoors can control the accumulation of moisture, cooking odors, and combustion by-products (a particularly important consideration for natural gas appliances). General guidelines call for a minimum of 100 cfm for kitchens. Manufacturers should supply a cfm rating for all exhaust fans. Experts generally recommend selecting fans based on an air pressure resistance of 0.25 or 0.30 inches of water rather than 0.1 inches. Kitchen design and cabinet layout affects exhaust fan feasibility and cost. For many sources of moisture, odors, and combustion products (i.e., dishwasher, sink, microwave, portable grill or skillet, toaster, toaster oven, coffee maker, etc.), or where kitchens are open to other rooms, range hoods are not effective and general ventilation must be used.

Don't Oversize

In hot and humid climates, an *essential measure* to control indoor relative humidity is not oversizing the air conditioning equipment. Using the whole building design approach will ensure that equipment is designed for the actual cooling load, taking account of energy-saving measures such as low-E glazing. Studies show that it takes nearly five minutes of continuous operation before an air conditioner begins removing moisture from the air. If the system is oversized, it "short-cycles" and seldom runs long enough to remove any humidity. This raises the indoor humidity level, making the home feel damp and clammy, which results in the occupants wasting even more energy by keeping the home too cold in an attempt to compensate. It also almost guarantees the growth of mold. Builders should be ready to address buyer anxiety about "undersized" air conditioning with facts and figures. This is one case where bigger is *not* better.

Air Movement

Some homes can be be sited and designed to take advantage of prevailing winds as a cooling and ventilation strategy. Windows, stairwells, and other elements can be located to encourage cross-ventilation throughout the house.

Casement windows have a 90% open area, whereas double hung or sliding windows have less than a 50% open area. Casement windows offer additional advantages because, when properly placed, they help channel breezes into and out of the house. Natural ventilation can help keep houses cool and comfortable at the beginning and end of the cooling season, thereby shortening the times when air conditioning is required.

Adding ceiling fans, which do an excellent job of efficiently moving air, can further reduce the days when air conditioning is needed. Using natural ventilation and ceiling fans together may enable homeowners to set their thermostats up to 4 degrees higher in the cooling season. A ceiling fan should have a minimum clearance of 10 inches between the ceiling and the fan to

Ceiling Fan Sizes	
Largest Room Dimension	Minimium Fan Dimension (inches)
12 feet or less	36
12–16 feet	48
16–17.5 feet	52
17.5–18.5 feet	56
18.5 or more feet	2 fans

provide adequate ventilation in a standard room with 8-foot ceilings. In rooms with higher ceilings, fans should be mounted about 8 feet above the floor. Use ceiling fans with an ENERGY STAR® rating, and remember that ceiling fans cool people, not spaces. They generate heat when they operate and should be shut off when not in use. Occupancy sensors can guarantee this.

Air Sealing

Air sealing is discussed fully in Chapter 3, The Building Envelope, "Insulation and Air Sealing." Air sealing also affects indoor environmental quality in several ways:

Controlling humidity. Air sealing reduces leakage, which avoids excessively dry indoor conditions in winter. It also allows the home to stay dehumidified in hot, humid weather, avoiding mold growth and clammy indoor conditions.

Preventing mold growth. Air sealing helps minimize the random flow of air through the building envelope. This in turn minimizes the chances that humid air (from inside in winter or outside in hot-humid conditions) will contact and wet a cold surface, with the potential of causing mold growth if the condition persists for long periods.

Reducing drafts. Indoor environmental quality is improved substantially if drafts are eliminated in winter conditions. This is reflected in the design of air distribution systems, which can be simpler and more effective if they don't have to compensate for drafts.

Acoustics

Noise can be considered a pollutant. Builders who want to guarantee exceptional indoor environmental quality must plan, design and construct homes carefully to manage this potential issue.

Outside the House: Knowing the characteristics of your site (whether it is one home or a complete subdivision) is a great start and can eliminate the need to add sound-conditioning after your project is built. Remember to evaluate for both daytime and nighttime situations. High noise sources might be airports, military bases, freeways, business and entertainment districts, schools, or sports arenas. Locating your property in urban areas or close to public transportation, shopping and busy business districts can minimize the number of car trips and is considered very green, but may require extra attention for noise management because of the potentially higher noise levels.

Courtyards created by massing together buildings can be noisy, but designing them to have the open side away from the source of noise can improve the situation. Landscaping inside the courtyard can help minimize the amount of sound that reverberates within the courtyard.

Consider using the natural topography (or create hills and swales that are high enough to act as a barrier), sound barriers, other buildings or landscaping to help shield your project. Depending on your circumstance you may also want to think about the placement of future buildings that might reflect or reverberate sounds. The effectiveness of your barrier will depend on the frequency of noise and the angle of the 'sound shadow' and the effective height of the barrier. Higher frequencies are more effectively attenuated by barriers than are low frequency sounds. Even the densest landscaping placed between the source of noise and the home will only reduce noise slightly.

Inside the Home: Builders can help control noise by isolating sources of noise (appliances, machinery, etc.) in rooms that have been enclosed using sound absorbing strategies. Sound insulation (wall and duct systems) can reduce sound transmission from room to room through walls, floors and ceilings. Sound absorbing materials such as carpeting and acoustical ceiling tiles can also be designed into the home.

We have more and more high-tech gadgetry (big screen TV's, computer game equipment, CD players, and music systems) and homes that regularly include offices, media centers, multiple car garages that double as workshops, laundry rooms and kitchens large enough to hold commercial stoves and refrigerators means a potentially huge amount of noise to be managed. Here are some strategies to consider:

- Use interior solid core doors with acoustical seals;
- Consider insulating joist cavities;
- Consider resilient furring channels on the bottom of floor joists;
- Caulking can reduce air infiltration, and therefore noise, from the outside;
- Insulate around and under tubs and shower stalls;
- Keep pipes away from sensitive rooms such as bedrooms, office or media rooms.

Avoiding air leakage. Relatively small air leaks can transmit sound very efficiently through partitions. It is important first to block air leaks between adjacent rooms before investing in measures that reduce sound conduction. The most common leaks are through doorways, around electrical outlets and under the wall sill plate.

Conduction through walls. In general, the conduction of higher-frequency sound (high-pitched voices, music, etc.) can be suppressed by isolating the wall surfaces from each other. One common method is to hang the gypsumboard on one side of the wall on acoustical channels. Another method is to use separate studs for each side of the wall. It helps to insert cellulose or fiber glass within the wall. Any insulation in the wall cavity will help reduce sound transmission. Concrete and masonry also reduce sound transmission.

Transmission through floors. In addition to closing off leaks and suppressing high-frequency air-borne sound with isolation, impact noise needs to be controlled in floor systems. This can be done by inserting an impact-absorbing layer under the flooring.

Sound through ductwork. When acoustical isolation is important, ducts should be relatively long, and should be lined with acoustical duct liner. Locate air handling units carefully to avoid noise pollution in areas of concern, such as bedrooms. Design the ductwork and locate the interior air handler or furnace to minimize noise transmission to living spaces.

Equipment-generated sound. One common source of annoying sound is the compressor for the air conditioning unit. This device has a fan and a compressor, both of which can create noise.

Appliance-generated sound. While most modern dishwashers and refrigerators are remarkably quiet, energy-efficient, higher-cost units tend to be *very* quiet, an added plus to their efficiency and style.

Planning for acoustics. Home buyers typically are influenced by their initial impression, and so can be "wowed" by large, continuous open spaces. Open plans have their place, but having at least two living spaces that can be acoustically separated is a useful strategy when raising children, especially teenagers, or when there are two unrelated people sharing a house. This amenity needs to be pointed out to potential buyers.

Bath fans. Larger fans generally cost more but also last longer, run quieter, and allow for placement farther away from the living area, which in turn lessens noise problems.

Light Intensity and Quality

Energy-efficient lighting and daylighting tips are discussed in Chapter 4, Energy Efficiency, "Lighting." The intensity and quality of lighting are design issues that have an impact on environmental quality. Typically, a low level of background lighting, possibly indirect, should be coupled with focused "task lighting" that illuminates reading and work areas. It is both energy-wasting and unpleasant to over-light a large area, although many people rely on bright lighting to be able to see. Lighting controls are important, to allow selected lights to be dimmed or turned off. For example, it is desirable to be able to turn down the lights over the food preparation area while eating, if (as is very common in today's plans) the cooking and eating areas are in the same space.

Fireplaces and Stoves

Wood-burning fireplaces and stoves may be replaced by less polluting and more efficient gas or electric units. A typical gas fireplace is a sealed combustion unit. If a wood stove does not draw in its own combustion air, a supply of outside air near the stove is essential to prevent the stove's exhaust from backdrafting other appliances. A wood-burning fireplace should always have a separate supply of outside air delivered into the firebox, preferably inside a set of glass doors that can be closed to improve efficiency. Check local codes, as this may be required.

Sealed Combustion Furnaces or Boilers

Most furnaces are nondirect-vent units, meaning they use surrounding air for combustion. Other units are direct-vent (including power-vented and sealed-combustion) furnaces and include condensing models. They bring combustion air into the burner area via inlets that extend to the home's exterior. Condensing, sealed-combustion furnaces carry an installed-cost premium of around $500, but are preferred for efficiency and safety. Natural draft equipment is generally safe and approved by code. Nondirect-vent furnaces do have the potential to backdraft or otherwise leak carbon monoxide into the living space. If it occurs, which is rare, it can result in potentially serious health problems, injury, or fatality. As a last resort, furnace mechanical rooms can also be sealed from other rooms in the house. Insulate both the interior and exterior walls. Install two outside-air ducts (sized specifically for the furnace) from outside into the furnace room, with one opening near the floor and the other near the ceiling, or as otherwise specified by local codes.

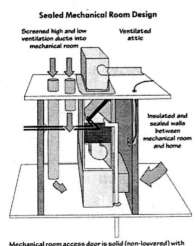

Sealed Mechanical Room Design

Screened high and low ventilation ducts into mechanical room

Ventilated attic

Insulated and sealed walls between mechanical room and home

Mechanical room access door is solid (non-louvered) with weatherstripping and a tight threshold.

Sealed Combustion Water Heaters

If natural draft fuel-fired water heaters are located in interior spaces, such as interior mechanical rooms connected to conditioned spaces or laundry rooms, consider providing air sealing and R-11 insulation. Also consider including provisions for outside combustion air, such as those shown in the illustration above. A simpler approach is to use a direct-vent water heater. Direct-vent units have a double flue pipe that includes both an intake for combustion air and a flue for exhaust gas. Note that some sealed combustion units do not operate as well in high wind areas. Sealed combustion water heaters carry a cost premium of approximately $300 to $500. A more common and less expensive alternative to sealed combustion is "power-venting," where a fan creates a stronger draft that is secure against backdrafting. Because they use forced air blowers, some units can be vented out the sidewall of the home rather than through the roof. Many power-vented water heaters are more efficient than their natural draft cousins.

Bathroom Exhaust Strategies

Bath exhaust fans can be set to a timer or hard wired for 24-hour operation as part of a whole house ventilation strategy. Whenever possible, select a fan that has been tested to deliver its rated output under normal conditions. Also, the high-efficiency motors used in quiet "low-sone" fans will use less electricity when operated continuously and are nearly silent. All bath fans should be vented to the outdoors and not discharged into an attic or crawlspace, where the moisture exhausted can cause serious damage to the home's structure.

Indoor Environmental Quality – Rules of Thumb

👍 Alternatives to traditional attached garages, such as detached garages or locked, vented storage spaces, help prevent exhaust gas and chemical gases and vapors from entering the home.

👍 Pursue moisture control techniques to minimize mold growth.

👍 Open-hearth fireplaces are not recommended. Installed fireplaces should have their own appropriately sized, direct-air supply, as well as tight-fitting glass doors.

👍 Fuel-fired appliances, furnaces, and water heaters should be located in insulated spaces that are outside the air envelope of the living area.

👍 Consider upgrading the air infiltration systems by using pleated, electro-static, electronic, or HEPA filtration.

👍 To reduce offgassing, use tacks rather than adhesives when securing carpet.

👍 Rough-in or install radon venting systems.

Additional Resources

"Air Sealing," *Technology Fact Sheet*, Office of Building Technology, State and Community Programs, Energy Efficiency and Renewable Energy,

U.S. Department of Energy. February 2000. 800-DOE-3732; www.eere.energy.gov/buildings/info/documents/pdfs/26448.pdf

Builder's Guide to Energy Efficient Homes in Georgia, Southface Energy Institute, Inc., Atlanta, Georgia. September 1999.

A Guide to Developing Green Builder Programs, NAHB Research Center. February 2000.

The Carpet and Rug Institute (CRI) Indoor Air Quality "Green Label" initiative encourages manufacturers to decrease chemical emissions from carpet to very low ranges; www.carpet-rug.com

The Resilient Floor Covering Institute (RFCI) has a certification program FloorScore™ for low-emitting resilient flooring; www.rfci.com

The GREENGUARD® Environmental Institute offers IAQ certification for low VOC-emitting wallcoverings.

Web Resources

www.energybuilder.com
    The Building Environmental Science and Technology Web site
www.epa.gov/iaq/homes/index.html
    The U.S. Environmental Protection Agency Web site
www.epa.gov/iaq/radon/zonemap.html
    Provides the EPA's radon zone map referenced earlier in this chapter.
www.lungusa.org/site
    The American Lung Assocation's indoor air quality information.
www.toolbase.org/index.aspx
    Toolbase: Indoor Environmental Quality
www.greenguard.org
    The GREENGUARD® Environmental Institute
www.mysoundchek.com
    "Putting a Check on Sound in Your New Home"
www.naima.org
    "Sound Advice for Today's Families."

Interactions

See the following chapters for information on how Indoor Environmental Quality affects other building considerations:

Chapter 7 Materials

Selecting Green Materials

Optimizing material selection is a key component of building a green home that minimizes its use of resources while providing improved energy performance and better indoor environmental quality. Environmentally friendly building materials are a growing and dynamic field, with more choices available every year. This chapter will address key issues and approaches to material selection and will refer builders to more detailed discussions, tools, and listings of materials.

Material selection is a complex process involving many variables, and there is rarely one best method that can be used across the board to select materials. Green material selection typically involves an assessment of a product's life cycle environmental impacts. This process tracks the raw materials used to produce a material, its production process, its transportation, its characteristics in use, and its disposal, reuse, or recycling options. Through the life cycle assessment process, a number of green attributes have been identified for various construction materials. The following attributes are included as an introduction to key green factors that builders should consider when assessing different construction products.

Renewability refers to materials that are derived from biological resources such as trees and agricultural products. Examples include natural linoleum, cork, bamboo, straw-based board products (equivalent to cabinet-grade particleboard or medium-density fiberboard), and wood and engineered wood products. Some may be biodegradable at the end of their useful life.

Recycled content includes both *post-consumer* and *pre-consumer* (also known as *post-industrial*) content. Materials with recycled content are available for many types of building products, often with competitive, comparable, or better performance than materials made from virgin materials. Post-consumer content, which refers to materials that have been recovered from home or office waste streams, provides greater environmental benefits than pre-consumer/post-industrial.

Reusability/recyclability describes how easily a product may be reused or recycled once it has reached the end of its service life. Products that can be more easily disassembled or separated from adjacent materials for reuse or recycling should be considered. Look for products that are collected by recycling centers, such as cardboard, glass, plastics, or metal, or that come from manufacturers sponsoring take-back programs for their materials.

Durability of a material describes what the expected maintenance and service life of a product may be in a given environmental exposure. Low-maintenance products with long service lives are typically preferred by home buyers and merit particular attention, although they may contain large amounts of embodied energy as illustrated in the next section.

Embodied energy is the energy required to extract, process, package, transport, install, and recycle or dispose of materials that make up the building. Up to 70% of the total energy invested in a building's construction is embodied in the materials themselves. Because the energy consumed to transport materials is often a significant portion of its embodied energy, locally produced materials are preferable to materials that must be shipped long distances.

MATERIAL	EMBODIED ENERGY	
	MJ/kg	MJ/m3
Aggregate	0.10	150
Straw bale	0.24	31
Soil-cement	0.42	819
Stone (local)	0.79	2030
Concrete block	0.94	2350
Concrete (30 Mpa)	1.3	3180
Concrete precast	2.0	2780
Lumber	2.5	1380
Brick	2.5	5170
Cellulose insulation	3.3	112
Gypsum wallboard	6.1	5890
Particle board	8.0	4400
Aluminum (recycled)	8.1	21870
Steel (recycled)	8.9	37210
Shingles (asphalt)	9.0	4930
Plywood	10.4	5720
Mineral wool insulation	14.6	139
Glass	15.9	37550
Fiberglass insulation	30.3	970
Steel	32.0	251200
Zinc	51.0	371280
Brass	62.0	519560
PVC	70.0	93620
Copper	70.6	631164
Paint	93.3	117500
Linoleum	116	150930
Polystyrene Insulation	117	3770
Carpet (synthetic)	148	84900
Aluminum	227	515700

NOTE: Embodied energy values based on several international sources - local values may vary.

Environmental impact can be considered in two ways. In one respect, it refers to the effect a material has on the indoor environmental quality within a home. In a broader context, it refers to a material's effect on the outdoor environment and atmosphere. To create a healthy indoor environment, select materials that limit offgassing, have minimal or no toxic properties, and do not shed dust or fiber. For the outdoor environment, select materials that minimize impacts on ozone depletion and global warming (e.g., products that do not contain HCFCs, halons, etc.) and minimize the release of toxic waste.

Material Reuse

Consider reusing lumber scraps such as 2x wood cutoffs for bridging, stakes, bracing, shims, drywall nailers, and blocking. Similarly, cutoff sheathing waste can be used for drywall stops and furring.

Consider setting up an in-place concrete recycling system (to create aggregate) in larger projects.

Misordered, excess, or slightly damaged finished building products can be reused at the jobsite, donated for a tax deduction to nonprofit building supply centers, or transported to another jobsite. The same may be true for commodity items such as drywall and framing, if they are not damaged and if an outlet for used building materials is available.

Reuse packaging materials whenever possible. For example, reuse cardboard for your packing and transportation needs. Some product manufacturers also take back pallets or other packing materials for reuse or recycling.

How to Find Green Material Suppliers

Green building product information can be found in periodicals, books and other resource guides, and Web sites. A number of organizations monitor the market for new products, evaluate the performance of new and evolving products, and—perhaps most important—identify green product suppliers. Two leading resources are the *Environmental Building News' GreenSpec* and the National Center for Appropriate Technology's (NCAT) *Guide to Resource Efficient Building Elements.*

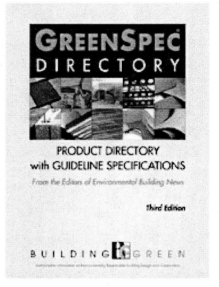

For more information, contact *Environmental Building News* (802-257-7300; www.buildinggreen.com) and NCAT's Center for Resourceful Building Technology (406-549-7678; www.crbt.org).

In the GreenSpec Directory, the editors of *Environmental Building News* have carefully screened information on more than 1,750 green building products. Here you will find product descriptions, environmental characteristics and considerations, and manufacturer contact information organized according to the 16-division CSI MasterFormat™ system. The directory listings cover more than 250 categories of building products. The GreenSpec Directory does not rely on any industry or manufacturer fees for production. Information included in the document is dependable and unbiased.

Both the GreenSpec Directory and NCAT Guide have extensive materials information and supplier listings and have served as sources for some of the descriptions provided below.

Green Materials by Category

Green products and systems are continually coming onto the market. The pages that follow contain a limited listing of green products that have been used for a number of years.

Foundations

Concrete containing recycled waste (slag cement, flyash, aggregate). Concrete with flyash and other recycled waste can be cost competitive with regular concrete and is available in many locations. Concrete with flyash sets up somewhat more slowly, but is easy to work with and has a slightly smoother finish. Flyash can typically replace 15% to 25% of the Portland cement in a conventional concrete mix (in some cases, the replacement rate can be 35% or higher). Slag cement can typically replace 30% to 70% of the Portland cement in a concrete mix. Aggregates (typically sand and gravel) are mixed with water and cement to make concrete. Recycled concrete or other recycled materials can be used as aggregate in new concrete. Recycled concrete is frequently crushed and used as fill material.

Insulating Concrete Forms (ICFs). Lightweight, interlocking, rigid foam blocks or panels can be used as a permanent concrete form for foundations. These hollow assemblies are filled with reinforced concrete similar to traditional concrete foundations. However, the foam forms remain in place, acting as high-performance insulation and as an attachment point for finishes. Because of the modular nature of the blocks and the known volume of concrete inside them, little waste of either material is generated. Concrete is a locally derived material and can incorporate recycled or post-industrial by-products such as flyash or slag cement.

Insulated concrete forms (Photo courtesy of www.austinenergy.com)

Insulating Precast and Poured Concrete. Recently, other insulating concrete wall systems have come onto the market, including precast and insulated cast-in-place assembles.

Non-asphalt based damp proofing. Synthetic rubber and cement-based damp proofing products are available that do not contaminate soil and ground water. Polyethylene-based damp proofing products typically contain a significant percentage of post-consumer recycled materials.

Frost-Protected Shallow Foundation (FPSF). A frost-protected shallow foundation (FPSF) is a green technology that conserves resources, reduces disturbance of the soil, speeds construction, and reduces construction costs by several thousand dollars on a typical house. In the past, most buildings in cold climates have been protected from frost damage by starting the foundation below the frost line or in solid rock. In contrast, FPSFs use polystyrene insulation board to retain heat under foundations, and in that way, to raise the frost line. FPSFs as little as 12 inches below grade are protected from damaging frost heave, even where the design frost depth is 15 feet or more.

FPSFs for heated buildings keep ground temperatures above freezing by retaining heat from the building. FPSFs for unheated buildings and structures have insulation under the entire slab and foundation wall and extending several feet beyond. Thicker insulation is used to retain heat that is in the deep ground below the structure and can be used on attached garages,

porches, and freestand-
ing buildings, posts,
and walls.

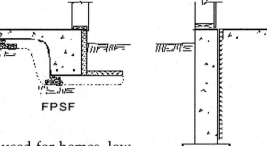

FPSF

Conventional

FPSF designs are avail-
able for slab-on-grade
foundations, crawl-
spaces, and walk-out
basements. They are widely used for homes, low-
rise apartments, and commercial buildings as
well as remodeling additions.

More than 1.5 million FPSFs have been built in the United States, Canada,
and Scandinavia over the past 50 years. U.S. research and development
has been conducted by the NAHB Research Center under grants from the
Society of the Plastics Industry, the U.S. Department of Housing and Urban
Development, and the U.S. Department of Energy's National Renewable
Energy Laboratory. Necessary climate data has been prepared by the
National Climatic Data Center of the National Oceanic and Atmospheric
Administration (NOAA) working with the NAHB Research Center.

Walls and Floors

Engineered lumber. Manufactured laminated veneer lumber, laminated
strand lumber, glue-laminated lumber, and I-joists offer consistent performance, predictable quality, and superior structural characteristics. Engineered lumber consists of wood veneers and strands combined with adhesives to produce practical and economical alternatives to solid wood framing
in headers, beams, and joists. Engineered lumber techniques include the following:

- **Substitute engineered lumber for 2 x 10s or larger.** While I-joists have
  slightly more embodied energy than dimension lumber, they are manufactured from underutilized wood species and forest thinning.
- **Use engineered lumber for headers and beams.** Manufactured laminated veneer lumber and laminated strand lumber are stronger than
  dimension lumber of the same size and are well-suited to replace solid or
  built-up headers.
- **Use wood I-joists for floors and ceilings.** I-joists have a high strength-
  to-weight ratio and provide structural support for floors and roofs, while
  only using one third of the material required for traditional solid joist
  systems.

Light gauge steel framing. Steel framing (studs and floor systems) has many
advantages: it contains a minimum of 25% recycled material and is 100% recyclable. There is typically less scrap and waste; a steel frame house accounts
for little more than 1 cubic foot of steel scrap. Steel is noncombustible and is
not vulnerable to termites and mold and therefore may contribute to improved indoor air quality. Steel framing can be substituted "stick for stick,"
or specific "steel techniques" can be employed to use less steel. Substituting

Steel framing is increasingly popular in residential construction.

steel for wood is appropriate in non-load-bearing interior partitions. Standard details and load tables are available online at www.steelframing.com. Pay attention to ensure a thermal break is provided to avoid energy losses and moisture problems that can be associated with thermal bridging. A finished house with steel framing does not appear different from any other home. One great advantage is that the framing will not deflect, bend, or warp over time.

Structural insulated panels (SIPs) for walls and roofs. SIPs are most often OSB sheathing laminated to expanded polystyrene foam cores and are designed to take the place of traditional stick framing. The product is produced in large panels, which can be ordered from the manufacturer in standard or custom sizes with window and door openings already cut in place. SIPs create energy-efficient, quiet homes due to tight construction and the uniformity of the insulation layer. Initial savings in framing and the labor typically required to insulate and gap seal may be offset by learning curve costs or slightly higher material costs.

Autoclaved cellular concrete (ACC). ACC is a lightweight, precast concrete product typically manufactured as blocks or panels. The ACC process uses steam-cured hydrogen bubbles to create an insulating material that can be worked with regular tools. A typical solid 8-inch ACC block achieves R-8 and also has thermal mass benefits.

Insulating Concrete Forms (ICFs). ICFs are foam insulation formwork for reinforced concrete walls. These permanent forms stay in place after the initial pouring of the concrete core, providing insulation, finish attachment surfaces, and a chase for utilities. ICFs typically accept all traditional finishes, including siding, stucco, brick, plaster, and drywall. Benefits to the homeowner include high thermal and acoustical performance, low air filtration, disaster and termite resistance, and extremely long durability. Construction costs for ICF homes average about 2% to 5% more than traditionally framed homes. Lightweight, interlocking blocks or panels are easily cut-to-fit with common hand-tools and set in place with little to no waste. ICF construction training is readily available through regional manufacturers.

Concrete Floors. Intermediate floors in homes can be constructed of conventionally formed concrete, concrete on steel deck, concrete on steel joists, concrete on fiber glass joists, precast hollow-core plank, or ACC.

Forestry and Lumber Programs

SFI-certified lumber program. The Sustainable Forestry Board's Sustainable Forestry Initiative® program is a comprehensive system of principles, objectives, and performance measures developed by professional foresters, conservationists, and scientists (among others) that combines the perpetual growing and harvesting of trees with the long-term protection of wildlife, plants, soil, and water quality. There are currently over 150 million acres of forestland in North America enrolled in the SFI® program, making it among the world's largest sustainable forestry programs.

FSC-certified lumber. The Forest Stewardship Council (FSC) certification system ensures that an independent evaluation has been performed on a forest company's practices based on rigorous, publicly available forest management standards. These include long-term economic viability, protection of biodiversity, conservation of ancient natural woodland, long-term responsible management, recognition of indigenous peoples' and forest workers' rights, and regular monitoring. The FSC verifies claims from the forest to the final product, a process known as "chain of custody" monitoring. Select lumber and other forest products that carry the FSC registered trademark whenever possible in order to support responsible forestry and provide forest owners with an incentive to maintain and improve forest management practices.

Wall Cladding / Exterior Finishes

Recycled-content siding. Alternatives to wood siding include siding with recycled content, such as aluminum and wood fiber. Aluminum siding has high recycled content and is itself recyclable but has high embodied energy. Engineered and composite wood siding is a combination of post-industrial wood fiber and resin. Coating and pre-finishing the siding enhances weather resistance and durability. When choosing siding, seek recycled products that use post-industrial scrap in the manufacturing process.

Fiber-cement siding and exterior trim. Fiber-cement siding and trim is durable, impact resistant, moisture resistant, and termite resistant. It also inhibits fungus growth, is noncombustible, and is easy to install and finish. Installers must be careful when sawing the material. Masks are recommended to avoid inhaling harmful dust and particles.

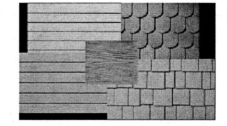

Engineered wood trim. Exterior wood trim material is available in finger-jointed and glued stock fabricated from several species of wood, such as pine and redwood. These materials are made from smaller pieces of wood, allowing the use of smaller, sustainably harvested trees. These products are typically available preprimed, thus ensuring durability and saving labor.

Recycled plastic lumber. Recycled plastic lumber is produced in a wide variety of sizes and colors for use in decks, fences, landscaping, countertops, and exterior furniture. Most are made from 90% to 100% post-consumer plastics such as HDPE and LDPE, while composite products are made from post-consumer plastics and wastewood fibers. Avoid using virgin plastic lumber. All recycled plastic lumber should have a label prominently displayed.

Traditional Portland Cement Stucco. Traditional Portland Cement Stucco (not to be confused with EIFS, which, unlike stucco, does allow moisture to escape) can be applied to masonry, concrete, or framed walls. Stucco is made from materials that are extracted and manufactured regionally.

Patios vs. decks. Patios may be more environmentally friendly than decks, because they require fewer materials and resources to construct. When built out of bricks, concrete, or traditional masonry, patios are more durable and weather resistant and typically require less maintenance. For decks, consider the following options: recycled plastic lumber and recycled wood–polymer composite lumber (both products look good and are far more durable and low-maintenance than wood); reclaimed, decay-resistant woods such as reclaimed redwood; or sustainably harvested, decay-resistant woods.

Roofs

Light-colored roofing. Some light colored roofing materials can increase solar reflectance values, meaning more of the sun's energy is reflected and less absorbed into the home. This can reduce cooling requirements by as much as 20%. Higher solar reflectance can be achieved with light-colored roofing materials such as tiles, painted metal, shingles, and white-reflective membranes and coatings.

Recycled-content organic asphalt shingles. Recycled-content organic asphalt shingles have characteristics similar to those of fiber glass asphalt shingles; they are lightweight and come with warranties of up to 30 years. However, they also contain recycled waste paper and/or use reclaimed mineral slag in their aggregate surface.

Long-lasting roofing: tile and slate. Tile and slate roofing materials are very durable, are easy to maintain, and have good fire ratings. Larger structural systems may be required to support the higher weight of tile and slate.

Metal roofing. Metal roofing made from steel, aluminum, or copper is durable and low maintenance. The components come in many sizes and shapes, including panels, shingles, shakes, and tiles. Some products contain up to 100% recycled material, and many products can be recycled. Avoid metal roofing where lead is used in the alloy or coating.

Insulation and Air Sealing

When sealing duct work joints, mastic is the best choice. If using tape, make sure it meets UL-181.

Air sealing materials. Look for low-VOC compounds, specifically, caulk, sealant, glue, tape, mastic, spray foam, and other related products. For large penetrations, consider reduced toxicity spray foams rather than batt insulation. Use noncombustible sealants between floors and between the living space and attic. Installers should check with the manufacturers for safe work practices when installing insulation.

Insulation Types

Batt Insulation
- Least expensive option
- Look for 30% recycled content.
- Always include sealing to reduce air flow.
- Check VOC offgassing rating to get lowest levels.

Blown-in Insulation
- Spray or dry pack
- More than 80% recycled content for cellulose (20 - 25% for fiber glass)
- Helps reduce infiltration.
- Insist on borate-treated cellulose only, not ammonium sulfate.
- Fiber glass or cellulose or rock wool

Rigid Foam
- Typically closed cell installed on the exterior as sheathing
- Good for reducing heat loss/gain through studs
- Can serve as moisture drainage plane (with proper installation!)
- Used in wall, roof, and basement applications

Spray Foam
- Very high R-values possible
- Excellent for sealing the envelope tightly
- Great for irregular spaces
- Most expensive option
- Available in low or high density

Recycled Cotton Batts
- Made from recycled blue jean material
- Doesn't "itch"
- No IAQ problems
- Limited availability
- Potentially expensive

Windows

The National Fenestration Rating Council (NFRC) Web site (www.nfrc.org) is a valuable resource for builders. The NFRC-certified rating or label describes certain physical properties of the entire window, not just the glass: the U factor, the Solar Heat Gain Factor (SHGF), and the Visible Transmittance (VT). Air leakage data may also be provided from another source (see Chapter 2, Renewable Energy, Passive Solar Design Strategies for more extensive discussion).

The wide array of more environmentally friendly window frames and glazing products is described below.

Window frames. Some builders prefer the look and feel of wood window frames, while others prefer the lower maintenance of aluminum or vinyl frames. Clad frames with wood interiors and a thin, more weather-resistant cladding on the exterior are an excellent green choice because they combine the advantages of wood and vinyl or metals. For energy efficiency reasons, non-thermally broken metal frames are not typically recommended, unless you are building in a climate with mild winters. In other climates, metal frames must have a thermal break sash, and frames made of "pultruded fiber glass" are gaining in popularity.

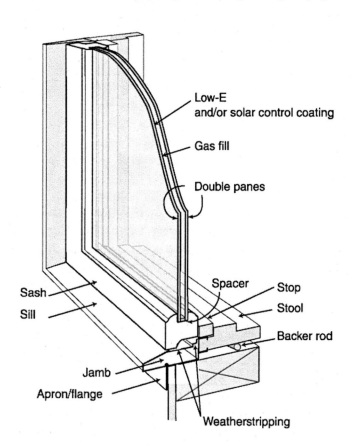

Sash
Sill

Low-E and/or solar control coating

Gas fill

Double panes

Spacer   Stop
                Stool

                Backer rod

Jamb

Apron/flange

Weatherstripping

Energy-efficient window technologies are available to produce windows with the U-factor, SHGC, and VT properties needed for any application.

High-performance window glazing. For most climates, double-pane windows are essential to reduce heat loss or heat gain. Other glazing options that increase thermal performance include low-emissivity (low-e) films that reflect heat into or away from the building, depending on climate; argon or krypton gas, which is used between panes to lower conductivity and increase R-value; and "Heat Mirror," a clear low-e film used between window panes to create a greater number of insulative chambers within the window.

Light pipes: Light pipes transmit natural daylight into interior and otherwise dark spaces through highly reflective, insulated cylinders. Daylight is channeled to a light diffuser in the ceiling, which provides natural daylight, increases comfort, and enhances indoor environmental quality.

Energy Star®-rated windows are tailored to fit the energy needs of the country's three main climate regions: Northern, Central, and Southern.

Finishes

Low- or no-VOC (volatile organic compound) interior latex paint. Many latex paints are available with low amounts of organic solvent. Select latex paints that also have low or no VOCs. These paints have lower odors and emissions when wet or newly dried. Latex paint is generally nonflammable, has lower toxicity than oil-based paints, and can be cleaned up with water.

Low-VOC, water-based wood finishes. Water-based, formaldehyde-free, nonflammable, low-odor, and low-VOC content wood finishes are available in gloss, semi-gloss, satin, and solid finishes for interior applications. These products are easy to clean up as well as fast drying, which reduces down-time between coats.

Natural paint. Natural paints, made from milk protein, plant, or mineral-based compounds, can be a viable alternative to conventional paints. Natural paints are not necessarily low-VOC, as some types are organic and solvent-based, and contain isoaliphatic hydrocarbons. Some paints use citrus oil solvents, which dry quickly; however, they may cause allergies or irritation in environmentally sensitive individuals.

Recycled-content and/or formaldehyde-free interior panels. Choose from a variety of recycled-content and/or formaldehyde-free panel materials for millwork, cabinets, and paneling. These include formaldehyde-free medium density fiberboard (MDF), panels made from post-consumer and post-industrial corrugated boxes and newspapers, and panels made from agricultural waste such as wheat, straw, and soy. Some panels are available in sizes up to 5' x 18' with thicknesses of ¼" to 1¼".

Finger-jointed trim. Finger-jointed trim is made from short lengths of lumber formerly scrapped or burned for fuel. Finger-jointed trim will need to be painted, and some products have a hardwood veneer well suited for stain or other finishes.

Environmental considerations for selecting flooring. Environmentally preferable flooring materials have one or more of the following characteristics: they produce low emissions, are made from rapidly renewable and/or natural resources, contain recycled content, are recyclable, require little maintenance, and/or do not require toxic cleaners to maintain.

General carpet information. Carpet systems, including carpets, carpet cushions, and carpet adhesives, can emit significant levels of VOCs, particularly during and immediately after installation. The Carpet and Rug Institute of Dalton, Georgia, has established a Green Label testing program that sets emission thresholds for VOCs, formaldehyde, and other compounds found in carpets, cushions, and adhesives. Carpet selections should meet or exceed these standards. Carpet must also be properly maintained to control dust, antigens from dust mites, and potential microbial growth (often the result of excessive moisture from leaks, spills, etc.). Carpet cleaners should also use low-emission formulations where available.

Recycled-content carpet. Post-consumer products (such as soda bottles) containing polyethylene terephthalate (PET) are recycled into polyester carpet face fiber, thereby minimizing landfill waste, air pollution, and the fuel required for producing virgin fiber. PET is inherently stain-resistant and is more hydrophobic than nylon. Where additional durability is required, a growing number of nylon carpets are available that incorporate recycled content into their face fibers or backings.

For padding, consider synthetic felted pad made from carpet manufacturing waste, natural fiber wool or jute, foamed pads made from true natural rubber, or foamed pads manufactured without the use of ozone-depleting chemicals.

Flooring from rapidly renewable materials. Bamboo and cork flooring are long lasting, sustainable flooring alternatives. Controlled bamboo forests mature in three to five years and typically produce as much flooring as a hardwood forest does after 40 years. Installing bamboo is similar to installing hardwood floors. Cork flooring is harvested from the bark of the cork tree, which grows back completely in 9 to 14 years. Cork has natural fire resistance, is resilient, will not rot, is hypoallergenic, and provides insulation and cushioning. Cork wear layers can be waxed, varnished, and coated with polyurethane or acrylic.

Recycled-content ceramic tile. Recycled content ceramic tiles are available in a wide variety of styles, colors, and finishes. Installation and cost are often similar to non-recycled tiles. Some contain as much as 85% post-consumer recycled glass.

Natural linoleum. Natural linoleum is made primarily of natural raw materials: linseed oil, rosins, and wood flour combined with a natural jute backing. Linoleum is highly resistant and over time becomes harder and more durable, while remaining quiet and comfortable underfoot.

Materials — Rules of Thumb

👍 Consider, at a minimum, the following seven life-cycle analysis criteria when selecting green materials: recycled content, waste reduction, reusability/recyclability, renewability, durability, embodied energy, and air quality impacts.

👍 Refer to *GreenSpec,* the *Guide to Resource Efficient Building Elements,* and other resources to find suppliers and get the latest information on green building materials.

👍 Consider foundation materials that have recycled waste content (e.g., flyash).

👍 Select insulation with recycled content and/or other environmental benefits (e.g, low VOCs).

👍 Select high-performance window frames and glazing to minimize the home's heating and cooling loads. Consider light pipes for additional natural lighting.

👍 Select finishes that are formaldehyde-free, have low- or no-VOC content, and are low in organic solvents.

Case Study: Material Savings / Framing Techniques

Software: SoftPlan Systems, Brentwood, TN
Builder: Caruso Homes, Crofton, MD
House type: 2,300 square feet, single family detached

Estimating software was used to quantify the material savings of selected efficient framing techniques.

Technique	Savings[1]
Accurate take-off tools	$595
Increased spacing of floor joists from 12" to 19.2"	$412[2]
Modular roof design	$194
House configuration (modular overall dimensions)	$124
Reduced header sizes	$39

1 Savings based on lumber prices from mid-Atlantic region, March 1996.
2 Because the builder typically uses 3/4" floor sheathing, the increased joint spacing did not require thicker floor sheathing.

Source: NAHB Research Center's *Residential Construction Waste Management – A Builder's Field Guide.*

Case Study: Material Savings / Value-Engineering Techniques

Software: Argos Systems, Bedford, MA
Builder: DeLuca Enterprises, Newtown, PA
House type: 2,300 square feet, single family detached

Estimating software was used to quantify the material savings of selected value-engineering techniques.

Technique	Savings[1]
In-line framing spaced at 24" o.c.	$960
Increased spacing of floor joists from 16" to 24"	$747[2]
Reduced header sizes	$162
Relocating four windows and doors	$45
Ladder framing at intersecting walls	$45
Two-stud and backer corner framing	$30

1 Savings based on lumber prices from mid-Atlantic region, March 1996.
2 Because the builder typically uses 3/4" floor sheathing, the increased joint spacing did not require thicker floor sheathing.

Source: NAHB Research Center's *Residential Construction Waste Management – A Builder's Field Guide.*

  👍 Consider SFI- or FSC- or other (e.g., Canadian Standards Association) certified lumber with chain of custody whenever possible.

  👍 Use life-cycle analysis to select the greenest materials.

  👍 Consider reusing excess materials, such as cutoffs, in creative ways during the construction process.

  👍 Reduce and reuse material packaging as much as possible.

  👍 When selecting carpeting, at the very minimum, use Carpet and Rug Institute installation guidelines and select carpets, cushions and pads, and other materials with the Carpet and Rug Institute indoor air quality label.

  👍 To reduce offgassing, use tacks rather than adhesives to secure carpet.

Additional Resources

"Advanced Wall Framing," *Technology Fact Sheet*, Office of Building Technology, State and Community Programs, Energy Efficiency and Renewable Energy, U.S. Department of Energy. October 2000. 800-DOE-3732; www.eere.energy.gov/buildings/info/documents/pdfs/26449.pdf

Green Building Products 2nd edition, Alex Wilson and Mark Piepkorn, editors Co-published by BuildingGreen, Inc. and New Society Publishers, 2006; www.buildinggreen.com/ecommerce/

Guide to Resource Efficient Building Elements, Mumma, Tracy. National Center for Appropriate Technology's Center for Resourceful Building Technology, Missoula, Montana. www.crbt.org

The Environmental Resource Guide, The American Institute of Architects (AIA). John Wiley & Sons, Inc., 1 Wiley Drive, Somerset, NJ 08875. The AIA Environmental Resource Guide provides detailed life-cycle assessments of a number of construction materials. Updates are published on a biannual basis. 800-225-5945

Alternative Framing Materials in Residential Construction: Three Case Studies, NAHB Research Center. Labor and material cost analyses for SIPS, light-gauge steel, and welded-wire panels (shortcrete). Illustrated.

Environmental Building News monthly magazine. 802-257-7300; www.buildinggreen.com

Environmental Design and Construction magazine. 415-863-2614; www.edcmag.com/

Design Guide for Frost-Protected Shallow Foundations, 2nd Edition. NAHB Research Center. 800-638-8556

The Forest Products Marking program of CSA International demonstrates that forest products have originaated from a certified forest and have been verified through an independent chain of custody audit; www.csa-international.org/product_areas/forest_products_marking/

Web Resources

www.buildinggreen.com/
GreenSpec® - The 6th edition of GreenSpec® Directory includes information on nearly 2,000 green building products carefully screened by the editors of Environmental Building News. Directory listings cover

more than 250 categories-from access flooring to zero-VOC paints. Included are product descriptions, environmental characteristics and considerations, and manufacturer contact information with Internet addresses.

www.ebuild.com/
Published on the Web by Hanley Wood, LLC, the leading media company in the residential construction industry, ebuild is a comprehensive, interactive catalog that makes researching and comparing products fast and easy. Launched in February 2001, the Web site was created by and for building professionals.

www.p2pays.org/ref/08/07602.pdf
"Development of Cost-Effective, Energy-Efficient Steel Framing." U.S. DOE's Energy Efficiency and Renewable Energy Office of Industrial Technologies. Provides information on the benefits and applications of steel-framed construction.

http://mts.sustainableproducts.com/standards.htm
The Institute for Market Transformation to Sustainability: Sustainable Products Standards are Gaining Market Share

www.austinenergy.com/Energy%20Efficiency/Programs/
Green%20Building/Sourcebook/insulatedConcreteForms.htm
Contains extensive information about insulating concrete forms.

www.eere.energy.gov/buildings/tech/enveloperd/foundations.html
Contains good information about cast-in-place concrete, concrete or masonry blocks, insulating concrete forms, and permanent wood foundations.

www.greenguard.org
A global nonprofit organization with a scientific, third party board to establish environmental standards for indoor products and building materials.

www.recycle-steel.org
Web site of the Steel Recycling Institute. Contains facts about steel recycling, educational materials, and location of steel recycling locations all over America.

www.steel.org
Web site of the American Iron and Steel Institute. Contains useful information for builders.

www.steelframing.org
Contains useful information about steel use in homes and commercial buildings.

www.pathnet.org
An excellent repository of building materials, case studies, and innovative techniques.

www.greenbuilder.com/sourcebook/
The city of Austin's Green Building Network materials sourcebook.

www.oikos.com/green_products
Oikos Green Building Product Information, formerly the Resources for Environmental Design Index (REDI); updated frequently and CSI-categorized.

www.fscus.org/
Forest Stewardship Council U.S. Has information on FSC-certified lumber.

www.smartwood.org
SmartWood

www.greenseal.org
  Green Seal
www.aboutsfi.org/sfilabel.asp
  Sustainable Forestry Initiative: SFI® Labeling Program
www.epa.gov/cpg
  EPA Comprehensive Procurement Guidelines (CPG). The following products list is also helpful: www.epa.gov/epaoswer/non-hw/procure/products.htm
 www.crbt.org
  The online version of *Guide to Resource Efficient Building Elements*, Mumma, Tracy. National Center for Appropriate Technology's Center for Resourceful Building Technology, Missoula, Montana.
www.nfrc.org
  The National Fenestration Ratings Council Web site provides an industry-standard rating for use by manufacturers. Helpful window selection information is also available.
www.osbguide.com
  The Structural Board Association is a group of Oriented Strand Board (OSB) manufacturers.
www.wbdg.org
  The Whole Building Design Guide is a comprehensive resource to a wide range of building-related design guidance, criteria, materials, and technology.
www.greenconcepts.com/greenliving/
  Green Building Concepts offers green supplier listings and other green building information.
www.nrdc.org/cities/building/rwoodus.asp
  The Natural Resource Defense Council's *Efficient Wood Use in Residential Construction: A Practical Guide to Saving Wood, Money, and Forests* offers an overview of OVE and other money- and wood-saving techniques. Available on-line and in print. 1998.
www.consumerenergycenter.org/tips/index.html
  The California Energy Commission's Consumer Energy Center Web site has extensive information on materials, green building, and green living.
www.bfrl.nist.gov/oae/software/bees.html
  The National Institute for Science and Technology's Building for Economic and Environmental Sustainability (BEES) software helps builders identify green building products through a set of predefined life cycle criteria. Builders can choose which criteria they wish to apply.
www.cement.org/homes/
  Web site of the Portland Cement Association on all aspects of concrete in homes. Call (847) 966-9106 for more information.
www.coolmetalroofing.org
  The online source of information for cool metal roofing sponsored by the Cool Metal Roofing Coalition.
www.ecco.org
  The Environmental Council of Concrete Organizations provides bulletins on using concrete as part of a sustainable environment. Call (800) 994-3226.
www.cement.org
  Web site of the Portland Cement Association. Contains useful information on building with concrete and using flyash and slag cement with concrete.

www.forms.org

Web site of the Insulating Concrete Forms Association. Contains useful information on building concrete homes with ICFs. Call (847) 657-9730 for more information.

www.slagcement.org

Web site of the Slag Cement Association. Contains useful information on using slag cement in concrete.

www.fema.gov/plan/prevent/saferoom/residential.shtm

Web site of the Federal Emergency Management Agency. Provides information on constructing safe rooms.

www.simplyinsulate.com

Simply Insulate

www.habitat.org/env/restores.aspz

Habitat for Hunamity

www.buildingreuse.org

Building Materials Reuse Association

cwm.wbdg.org

Whole Building Design Guide: Construction Waste Management

Interactions

See the following sections for information on how Materials affect other building considerations:

Chapter 8   Operation and Maintenance

Now that you have taken the time to design and build a better home by incorporating a balanced, integrated package of green building strategies, it only makes sense to tell the home buyer all about it. Savvy buyers are looking for the same efficiencies and performance features they have come to expect in everything from cars to computers, and you are the builder who can offer those same attributes in a home. Now is the time to tell them!

Consider developing a brief, informative homeowner's manual to 1) describe the green features of the house, 2) supply information about how owners can maintain, repair, and even replace/recycle the components in their home, and 3) explain how the owner can stay comfortable and safe while minimizing energy, water, and maintenance costs. Much of this information is free from product manufacturers, local utilities and government offices, and nonprofit organizations. Builders should also provide homeowners all manuals for installed equipment (e.g., furnace, air conditioner, etc.), and control devices (e.g., programmable thermostats). The builder should offer to come back and commission the house (make certain that all systems are operating correctly) in the peak of the summer cooling season and winter heating season. Both inspections should include checks for excessive infiltration, comfort, and hot, warm, or moist spots.

The strategies below can serve as a starting point for content that can be included in a homeowner's operation and maintenance (O&M) manual. Some developers and builders have found it helpful to add listings of area parks, recreation facilities, stores, schools, government centers, etc. See the Additional Resources listing at the end of this chapter for more information.

What the Builder Can Do in the Design Process

Anticipate a maintenance schedule. All homes need maintenance, but selecting products that require periodic (rather than frequent or annual) maintenance helps the owner establish a regular schedule for upkeep. For instance, brick siding requires virtually no maintenance and can be part of a passive solar design strategy, whereas other siding options may need frequent painting or repair and would offer no passive solar or thermal mass benefits. Another example is using composite lumber for decking rather than traditional wood lumber. Whatever maintenance is anticipated for the house should be described in writing to the home buyer. Providing this information and lower maintenance products is likely to result in greater home buyer satisfaction and fewer callbacks.

Provide a homeowner's manual of green features and installed products. List the green features built into the home and the products included to make the home a safer, more comfortable place to live. Identify the benefits of each feature, so the homeowner will understand and appreciate the features' importance. Consider identifying how one feature relates to another (e.g., using energy-efficient lighting, appliances, and windows allowed for a smaller, more efficient air conditioner to be installed). Background information and diagrams may also be helpful.

Address storage of hazardous materials. Any cleaning supplies, paints, and other chemicals should be stored in an enclosed, vented area separated from the house. Consider providing information to the homeowner regarding the recycling and proper disposal of hazardous materials.

Provide recycling storage bins. Most millwork manufacturers include recycling centers in their cabinetry lines. It is also possible to economically install bins in existing cabinetry. Local solid waste agencies can provide guidance on the appropriate design of compost bins. The maximum cost is around $40 per linear foot. Also consider supplying a composting center for the homeowner or offering one as an option.

Provide information on HVAC operation and maintenance. Proper HVAC operation and maintenance can lead to significant savings and greater homeowner comfort. Most HVAC units should be serviced annually to maintain their efficiency. Replacing filters regularly is also important (see the Indoor Environmental Quality Tips in this chapter for more information). Consult your HVAC equipment manual for specific information.

Miscellaneous tips. Tell your home buyer about any special steps you have taken to facilitate future additions or green renovations, such as pre-plumbing for a solar hot water system or rough-ins for radon mitigation. Even telling a homeowner about your use of modular dimensions can be helpful to any future additions the homeowner may wish to make. Use nontoxic, low-VOC paint, stains, and finishes as much as possible, but especially in indoor areas. Many large paint manufacturers have added a line of low-VOC paints to their traditional product offerings. The performance and durability of these products is comparable.

What the Homeowner Can Do

Indoor environmental quality (IEQ) tips. IEQ tips range from placing doormats at all exterior doors to thorough dusting and vacuuming in order to minimize the amount of dust and dirt entering the home's ventilation system to replacing toxic solvents and cleaners with nontoxic alternatives. Selecting low-toxic cleaners safeguards health and protects the environment. Biodegradable kitchen and laundry soaps, bathroom cleaners, and other products are available in many stores and via the Web. See the Resources listing at the end of this chapter for additional information. To eliminate dust and allergens, homeowners should consider purchasing vacuum cleaners with microfiltration capabilities, especially high-efficiency particulate air (HEPA) filters. Another option is to consider buying pleated, electrostatic, HEPA, or electronic filters for the HVAC unit. Change air filters regularly. The interval (anywhere from 1 to 12 months) depends on the type of filter used, your local climate, and hours of HVAC operation. The EPA indicates in its publication, *Should I Have My Ducts Cleaned?* (www.epa.gov/iaq/pubs/airduct.html), that air ducts should not generally be cleaned in typical homes. The homeowner may choose to limit dust and allergens by using a hard floor covering (e.g., wood or concrete) instead of carpet.

Integrated pest management and landscaping tips. Integrated pest management combines sanitation, physical exclusion, and mechanical controls (traps, baits, etc.) with limited, targeted pesticides. Using IPM programs often leads to fewer pests, and cleaner and healthier homes.

Collect compost made from yard waste and manure from the local parks department, department of natural resources, or other municipal agency rather than buying compost at a store.

Prune shrubs and trees enough to allow air to flow freely to an HVAC unit, but leave enough to ensure that passive solar landscaping is maintained. See Chapters 1, 2, and 5 for additional information about the effects of landscaping on energy and water conservation.

Energy and water conservation tips:

- Keep your water heater set at 120 degrees F to prevent scalding and to conserve energy. If a higher temperature for washing clothes and dishes is desired, buy appliances with booster heaters. Because of scalding risks, the hot water heater should not be set at more than 140 degrees. For every 10 degrees that you lower your hot water heater temperature, you will save an estimated 13% on your hot water heating cost.
- Service your hot water heater annually to remove sediments and other materials that lower the unit's efficiency. Another technique is to drain a gallon of water from the bottom of the hot water tank monthly.
- Set your thermostat no lower than 78 degrees in the summer and no higher than 68 degrees in the winter.
- Use a programmable thermostat to raise the summer temperature in the house by 5 degrees or more during unoccupied hours (while at work or in the evening). Conversely, lower the house's temperature in the winter. Depending on climate, turning back the household thermostat 5 degrees for even 8 hours will result in energy savings of 6% to 10%.
- Use compact fluorescent bulbs in your house. They last more than 10 times longer than traditional incandescent bulbs and use approximately 35% less energy. Compact fluorescent bulbs generally cost more than standard incandescents, but the replacement and energy savings more than make up for the higher purchase price.
- Set your dishwasher to the Energy Saver or Light Wash mode as often as possible. Also use the Air Dry or No Heat Dry setting.
- If you must water your lawn or garden, do so at night or before 9 a.m. to maximize the benefits to your lawn and garden and to minimize evaporation losses. In many climates, lawns will go dormant if not watered in hot, dry weather and will recover in milder weather.
- If you have reversible ceiling fans, be sure to adjust them so they force warm air down in the winter and are moving in the opposite direction in the summer.
- Do not place furniture or other objects over HVAC registers. Do not place heat-generating appliances near the thermostat.

Miscellaneous tips. Check for termites around the exterior perimeter of the home and in the crawlspace (if there is one). Environmentally friendly treatments such as termite traps and borate solution sprays are available for termite and pest control. If signs of termites are found, call a professional for inspection and treatment.

O&M Recommendations for Homebuilders & Homeowners

Stephen Ashkin, President of the Ashkin Group, has over twenty-six years experience in the cleaning industry, and has been at the forefront of "green cleaning" since 1990. He recommends the following tips; www.ashkingroup.com.

The design and construction of homes can have an enormous impact on both occupant health and costs related to keeping the house clean. Some of the things that designers and construction companies should consider to reduce the impacts on occupant health and the environment as a result of cleaning can include:

- Selecting finishes that are easy to clean. While obvious, not all paints, fabrics, carpets, etc., are created the same and some require a lot more effort and cost from the homeowner to maintain.
- In geographies with hard water where the home is not being constructed with a water softener, it would be preferable to avoid using bathroom countertops made of soft stone or shower partitions made of clear glass, as removing hard water stains may require acidic cleaners which can permanently damage stone and glass.
- Design entry ways and landscaping to minimize berries, flowers, pollens and other materials from being tracked into the home. And, install a faucet so that the entry way can be periodically pressure-washed.
- If the house is carpeted, make sure that the homeowner knows how to care for the carpets. Directions should include keeping entryways clean, using high quality entryway mats both directly outside and inside all entrances, the use of a high quality vacuum cleaner preferably certified by the Carpet & Rug Institute, and periodic extraction cleaning (typically one time per year depending on the traffic and soil levels). And if possible, encourage the homeowner to install a high quality central vacuum system that is exhausted directly outdoors.
- Encourage frequent cleaning using technologies that effectively remove soils and minimize the use of chemicals and water. This might include the use of micro-fiber floor mops, dusters and cloths which do a superior job compared to traditional sponge or cotton floor mops, feather dusters and cotton cleaning cloths.
- Encourage homeowners to minimize the use of potentially hazardous chemical cleaners such as those that are known to cause respiratory irritation, burn eyes and skin, flammable, combustible or poisonous. This information is readily available on product labels.

Additional Resources

Environmental Building News Product Catalog, A joint publication of E Build, Inc. and *What's Working,* 1997/98, $59. This catalog provides environmental, cost, and availability information for over 70 building materials. The catalog is set up in a three-ring binder format for easy catalog growth. As with the well-known Sweet's catalog, product literature from the manufacturer is provided, but the editors' environmental profile of the product is also provided, based on their green material selection criteria. An environmental overview of each major building material category (following CSI classifications) starts each section of the catalog.

Green Building Resource Guide, John Hermannsson AIA Architect, Taunton Press, 1997, $37.95. The *Green Building Resource Guide* lists over 600 building materials. Names and addresses of suppliers are provided, along with a brief description of the product. Cost information is provided on a relative basis, as compared to similar conventional products. The *Guide* is also available on CD-ROM.

Consumer Guide to Energy Savings, Alex Wilson and John Morrill, American Council for an Energy-Efficient Economy, 2003. This book provides excellent tips on ways to conserve energy around the home. Tips on tightening up your house, heating and cooling more efficiently, lighting options, cooking, and food storage are included. Options ranging from simple things the homeowner can do at no cost to replacement of inefficient equipment is discussed.

The Green Pages: The Contract Interior Designers' Guide to Environmentally Responsible Products and Materials, Andrew Funston, Kim Plaskon Nadel, Jory Prober, New York, NY. Listings of environmentally responsible building materials from 536 manufacturers. Includes information on flooring, furnishings, fabrics, paints, appliances, lighting, and more.

The Borrower's Guide to Financing Solar Energy Systems, (DOE/GO-10098-660), Dr. Patrina Eiffert, National Renewable Energy Laboratory, Golden, CO. September 1998.

Consumers Reports has monthly and annual reports on appliances, HEPA filters and vacuums, lighting, etc.

Guide to Building Your Dream Home, Sara Lamia, Home Building Coach, Inc., September 2003.

Web Resources

www.floridaplants.com
    Although oriented to Florida, this site offers numerous books on all topics from drought-tolerant plants and grasses to landscape design to pest management. In addition to printed publications, there is good information about specific trees, plants, and grasses; soil, water, and light conditions; and disease control. A useful site whether or not you live in Florida.

www.gvrd.bc.ca
    Sponsored by the city of Vancouver, British Columbia, this site provides information on waste reduction with useful strategies for both the construction site and the homeowner.

www.portlandonline.com/osd/
    The city of Portland's Green Building Web site has an energy conservation tips page and homeowner tips.

www.emagazine.com/
    This is the Web site for *The Environmental Magazine*. This, too, is a broad-ranging resource that includes access to information on resource-efficient home operation systems and products.

www.oikos.com/
    In addition to being a useful site for builders who are trying to locate environmentally responsible building materials, the searchable database

provides homeowners with names and phone numbers of green products for use both within and outside the home. Among the types of the products listed are paving and landscaping materials, furnishings, floor coverings, paints, and stains. The library, bookstore, and back issues of *Energy Source Builder* magazine may also provide information of interest.

www.realgoods.com

The Real Goods catalog store offers a variety of resource-efficient home products ranging from composting bins to fluorescent lighting to biodegradable cleaning agents.

www.aceee.org/consumerguide/index.htm

American Council for an Energy-Efficient Economy has lots of information on its Web site and numerous publications that educate consumers and homeowners on how to live more environmentally and economically. 202-429-0781

www.ase.org/section/_audience/consumers

The Alliance to Save Energy's consumer Web page provides vivid (and sometimes animated) energy-efficiency and conservation tips. Web links and publications are also available. 202-857-0666

www.nrdc.org/cities/living/gover.asp

The Natural Resources Defense Council provides helpful environmental information, as well as maintenance, water efficiency, and energy tips for homeowners at www.nrdc.org/cities/building/default.asp Publications are also available. 212-727-2700

www.austinenergy.com

The City of Austin's Green Building Program is well-known for its builder information, but also offers valuable homeowner tips. Notable content includes fact sheets on air filters, recycling, and lead; other publications and information are also available. 512-505-3700

www.greenhome.org

GreenHOME contains homeowner tips, as well as information on two affordable, green home construction projects.

www.eere.energy.gov/buildings/info/homes/index.html

U.S. Department of Energy's Consumer Energy Information Web site. Contains information on appliances, HVAC, building design and maintenance, and other relevant topics.

www.energystar.gov

U.S. EPA: ENERGY STAR for New Homes

Interactions

See the following sections for information on how Operation and Maintenance affects other building considerations:

General References

Green Building Programs

The expanded market interest in green homes has driven an increase in the number of green building programs across the country. In general, the programs offer building professionals and home owners a system to measure or rate the "greenness" of a home building project. These programs also provide valuable information on the benefits of green bulding and of buying green-built homes. Some local programs offer resources and incentives and provide training.

National Programs

NAHB's *Model Green Home Building Guidelines* and the accompanying Green Home Building Checklist were developed in 2005. NAHB's goal was to move environmentally-friendly home building concepts further into the mainstream marketplace. The NAHB's *Guidelines* were designed as a tool kit for local associations to create new green home building programs and to help them expand and flourish. The NAHB's Guidelines are available for free download at www.nahb.org/gbg. The CD-ROM is included with this publication for your reference.

The U.S. Green Building Council is now pilot testing *LEED® for Homes* (LEED-H). This voluntary rating system, targeted to reach the top 25% of homes with best practices and environmental features, is expected to be formally released in late 2007. It is part of the suite of assessment tools offered by the USGBC. The pilot test began in August 2005. The *LEED® for Homes* checklist can be found at www.usgbc.org and is included with this publication for your reference.

With its focus on energy efficiency, the ENERGY STAR® Qualified Homes program, a joint national program of the U.S. Environmental Protection Agency and the U.S. Department of Energy, helps homeowners save money and protect the environment through energy efficient products and practices. Builders who produce homes can earn the ENERGY STAR® under the Qualified Homes program by meeting guidelines for energy efficiency set by the U.S. Environmental Protection Agency. For information, go to www.energystar.gov/index.cfm?c=bldrs_lenders_raters.pt_bldr

Local Programs

At last count, more than 60 local green building programs had been created by homebuilder associations, utilities, local governments, and non-profit groups, and there are many more ready to launch. All are sponosred by either local home builder associations, local governments, local utilities, nonprofit organizations, or spearheaded by a consortia of these groups. A short list of established local programs includes:

www.builtgreen.org
    Built Green® Colorado

www.southface.org/web/earthcraft_house/ech_main/ech_index.htm
    EarthCraft House™ (Georgia)

www.vermontbuildsgreener.org
    Vermont Builds Greener (VBG) Program

www.builtgreen.net
    BUILT GREEN™, King and Snohomish Counties, Washington State

www.austinenergy.com/Energy%20Efficiency/Programs/
Green%20Building/index.htm
    The City of Austin's (TX) Green Building Program®

Ways to Search for Other Green Building Programs

The list of residential green building programs is ever growing, with web sites and contact information in various stages of development. Below we have provided a list of web resources that will help you research programs or builders available in your area:

www.pathnet.org/sp.asp?id=20978
    The Partnership for Advancing Technology in Housing (PATH) provides a list of programs that certify homes as being green, or energy-efficient. Many of the programs identified on the PATH list are offered through utility companies that provide rebates and incentives.

www.nahbrc.org/
tertiaryR.asp?TrackID=&CategoryID=1801&DocumentID=2858
    The NAHB Research Center provides a list (circa 2002) of U.S. Residential Green Building programs, contacts, and websites.

thegbi.org/residential
    The Green Building Initiative™ works with local home builder associations across the country to develop locally-relevant green building programs. To find out more about green building in your hometown, click on the appropriate city on the map posted on their web site.

www.nahb.org/local_association_search_form.aspx

> The NAHB provides a searchable web index to find your local home builder association (HBA). Contact your local HBA directly to find out if it offers a program based on the NAHB's Model Green Home Building Guidelines.

www.usgbc.org/DisplayPage.aspx?CMSPageID=1554

> The USGBC has selected 12 LEED® for Homes Providers to provide technical, marketing and verification support to builders. During the program's pilot phase, these LEED® for Homes Program Providers will be responsible for selecting appropriate pilot projects and verifying that the homes are built to meet the requirements of the rating system.

www.usgbc.org/Chapters/ChapterList.aspx?CMSPageID=191&

> USGBC Chapters provide local green building resources, education, and leadership opportunities.

Green Building Checklists

Green building programs provide some degree of third-party verification for builders and consumers interested in delivering or occupying environmentally responsible homes. As previously noted, many of the programs offered through utility companies provide rebates and incentives to the builder and/or homeowner.

Most of the local programs listed on the previous page have developed checklists to help rate the green homes builders design and construct. One sample checklist provided in this publication was developed by builders from King and Snohomish Counties in the State of Washington. The BUILT GREEN™ program of King and Snohomish Counties certifies homes that are designed to provide homeowners with comfortable, durable, environmentally friendly homes that are cost-effective to own and operate. These resource-efficient homes are crafted to exceed local building codes and provide homeowners with years of healthy, quality living, while protecting the Northwest environment. The Built Green checklist can also be found at www.builtgreen.net/documents/Homebuilder%20Checklist.pdf.

The USGBC's *LEED® for Homes* checklist is provided in this publication for your reference. The checklist may be updated by USGBC during the pilot, so check the USGBC website; www.usgbc.org

The NAHB's *Model Green Home Building Guidelines* are included on CD ROM with this publication, and are also available for free download at www.nahb.org/gbg.

Built Green™ Checklist

Home Builder New Construction Checklist

Master Builders Association of King and Snohomish Counties, State of Washington

BUILT GREEN™ Version 2007

Project Address

Company Name

Action Item Number	Possible Points	CREDITS	Points
ONE-STAR REQUIREMENTS (25 points minimum)			
	required	All ê items plus orientation	★
	required	Program Orientation (one time only)	★
	required	Section 1: Build to "Green" Codes & Regulations	★
	required	Earn 25 points from Sections 2 through 5, any items	★
	required	Prepare/post a jobsite recycling plan (Action Item 1.1.1.10)	★
	required	Provide an Operations & Maintenance Kit (Action Item 1.1.1.5)	★
TWO-STAR REQUIREMENTS (100 points minimum)			
	required	Meet 1-Star requirements	★
	required	Earn 75 additional points from Sections 2 through 5, with at least 6 points from each Section	★
	required	Attend a Built Green™ approved workshop within past 12 months prior to certification	★
THREE-STAR REQUIREMENTS (180 points minimum)			
	required	Meet 2-Star requirements plus point minimum	★
	NEW req	Achieve 10% of minimum point requirements in each section	★
FOUR-STAR REQUIREMENTS (250 points minimum)			
	required	Meet 3-Star requirements plus point minimum	★
	required	3rd party verification required (See reference)	★
Site & Water	required	No zinc galvanized ridge caps, copper flashing or copper wires for moss prevention (See action item 2.1.5.12).	★
Site & Water	required	Landscape with plants appropriate for site topography and soil types, emphasizing use of plants with low watering requirements [drought tolerant] (See action item 2.2.1.3).	★
Site & Water	required	Use the most efficient aerator available for the faucets used.	★
Energy	required	Energy Star Homes or equivalent required (See action item 3.1.1.5)	★
IAQ	required	Use low toxic/low VOC paint on all major surfaces (except for PVA primer which is currently not available) (See action item 4.3.1.25)	★
IAQ	required	Ventilate with box fans in windows blowing out during drywall sanding and new wet finish applications	
Materials	required	Enroll project in King County Construction Works or provide equivalent waste prevention and recycling plan (See action item 5.1.1.1).	★
	required	**Choose one of the following:**	★
IAQ		Provide built in walk-off matt and shoe storage area	
IAQ		Use plywood and composites of exterior grade or with no added urea formaldehyde for interior uses	
IAQ		Develop a written healthy jobsite plan and educate workers on implementation (see handbook for more	
IAQ		Use high efficiency pleated filter of MERV 12 or better, or HEPA	
IAQ		Install sealed combustion heating and hot water equipment	
FIVE-STAR REQUIREMENTS (500 points minimum)			
	required	Meet 4-Star requirements plus point minimum	★
Site & Water	required	minimum of 25% of total points earned for Site & Water (see 4-star copy)	★
Site & Water	required	Amend disturbed soil with compost to a depth of 10 to 12 inches to restore soil environmental functions (See acti	★
Site & Water	required	Use pervious materials for at least one-third of total area for driveways, walkways, and patios (See action item 2.	★
Site & Water	required	Limit use of turf grass to 25% of landscaped area (See action item 2.2.1.2).	★
Site & Water	required	Avoid soil compaction by limiting heavy equipment use to building footprint and construction entrance (See action	★
Site & Water	required	Preserve existing native vegetation as landscaping (See action item 2.1.2.2)	★
Site & Water	required	Retain 30% of trees on site – For Greenfield developments only. (See action item 2.1.2.3)	★
Energy	required	Minimum R-26 for overall wall insulation.	★
Energy	required	Maximum average U-value for all windows of .30.	★
Energy	required	Advanced framing with double top plates (See action Item 3.1.3.7).	★
Energy	required	Pre-wire for future PV	★
Energy	required	75% minimum Energy Star light fixtures.	★
Energy	required	Alternate: In Lieu of above energy requirements demonstrate home energy performance 30% beyond code per action item 3.	★
IAQ	required	Detached or no garage OR garage air sealed from house with automatic exhaust fan (See action item 4.3.1.8).	★
IAQ	required	Use plywood and composites of exterior grade or formaldehyde free (for interior use) (See action item 4.3.1.19)	★
Materials	required	Achieve a minimum recycling rate of 70% of waste by weight.	★
Materials	required	Use a minimum of 10 materials with recycled content.	★

Built Green™ Checklist (continued)

SECTION ONE: BUILD TO GREEN CODES/REGULATIONS & PROGRAM REQUIREMENTS			
1.1.1.1	★	Meet Washington State Water Use Efficiency Standards	★
1.1.1.2	★	Meet Stormwater/Site Development Standards	★
1.1.1.3	★	Meet Washington State Energy Code	★
1.1.1.4	★	Meet Washington State Ventilation/Indoor Air Quality Code	★
1.1.1.5	★	Provide owner with operations and maintenance kit	★
1.1.1.6	★	Prohibit burying construction waste	★
1.1.1.7	★	Take extra precautions to not dispose of topsoil in lowlands or wetlands	★
1.1.1.8	★	When construction is complete, leave no part of the disturbed site uncovered or unstabilized	★
1.1.1.9	★	Dispose of non-recyclable hazardous waste at legally permitted facilities	★
1.1.1.10	★	Prepare jobsite recycling plan and post on site	★
1.1.1.11	★	1-3 Stars: Install CO detector (hardwired preferred) for all houses with a combustion device or attached garage	★
1.1.1.12	★	4-5 Stars: Install CO detector (hardwired required) for all houses with a combustion device or attached garage	★
1.1.1.13	required	See 5-3 Matrix Tab/Spreadsheet	★
		SECTION ONE TOTALS	n/a

SECTION TWO: SITE AND WATER			
SITE PROTECTION			
Overall			
2.1.1.1	10	Build on infill lot to take advantage of existing infrastructure, reduce development of virgin sites	
2.1.1.2	10	Build in a BUILT GREEN™ development	
2.1.1.3	3--5	Use low impact foundation system such as pin systems or post and pier for at least 50% of the foundation	
		Subtotal	
Protect Site's Natural Features			
2.1.2.1	3	Avoid soil compaction by limiting heavy equipment use to building footprint and construction entrance	
2.1.2.2	3	Preserve existing native vegetation as landscaping	
2.1.2.3	4	Retain 30% of trees on site	
2.1.2.4	4	Retain (or add) deciduous trees south of house	
2.1.2.5	4	Do not build near wetlands, shorelines, bluffs, and other critical areas	
2.1.2.6	2	If building near wetland, shorelines, bluffs and other critical areas, preserve & protect beyond code	
2.1.2.7	5--10	Set aside percentage of buildable site to be left undisturbed	
		Subtotal	
Protect Natural Processes On-Site			
2.1.3.1	2	Install and maintain temporary erosion control devices that significantly reduces sediment discharge from the site beyond code requirements	
2.1.3.2	3	Use compost to stabilize disturbed slopes	
2.1.3.3	3	Balance cut and fill, while maintaining original topography	
2.1.3.4	4	Limit grading to 15 feet all around, except for driveway access	
2.1.3.5	4	Amend disturbed soil with compost to a depth of 10 to 12 inches to restore soil environmental functions	
2.1.3.6	2	Replant or donate removed vegetation for immediate reuse	
2.1.3.7	2	Use plants donated from another site	
2.1.3.8	3	Grind land clearing wood and stumps for reuse	
2.1.3.9	3	Use a water management system that allows groundwater to recharge	
		Subtotal	
Impervious Surfaces			
2.1.4.1	7	Design to achieve effective impervious surface equivalent to 0% for 5 acres and above; <10% for less than 5	
2.1.4.2	3	Use pervious materials for at least one-third of total area for driveways, walkways, patios	
2.1.4.3	10	Bonus Points: Install vegetated roof system (e.g. eco-roof) to reduce impervious surface	
2.1.4.4	10	Bonus Points: Construct no impervious surfaces outside house footprint	
		Subtotal	
Eliminate Water Pollutants			
2.1.5.1	4	Protect topsoil on site for re-use	
2.1.5.2	1	Wash out concrete trucks into Ecopan storage containers	
2.1.5.3	1	Establish and post clean up procedures for spills to prevent illegal discharges	
2.1.5.4	1	Reduce hazardous waste through good jobsite housekeeping	
2.1.5.5	4	Provide an infiltration system for rooftop runoff	
2.1.5.6	2	Construct tire wash, establish and post clean up protocol for tire wash	
2.1.5.7	2	Use slow-release organic fertilizers to establish vegetation	
2.1.5.8	2	Use less toxic form releasers	
2.1.5.9	3	Use non-toxic or low-toxic outdoor materials for landscaping (e.g. plastic, least-toxic treated wood)	
2.1.5.10	4	Phase construction so that no more than 60% of site is disturbed at a time and to prevent adverse impacts on adjoining properties or critical areas	
2.1.5.11	5	No clearing or grading during wet weather periods	
2.1.5.12	2	No zinc galvanized ridge caps, copper flashing or copper wires for moss prevention	
		Subtotal	

Built Green™ Checklist (continued)

WATER PROTECTION

Outdoor Conservation

2.2.1.1	2	Mulch landscape beds with 2 in. organic mulch	
2.2.1.2	5	Limit use of turf grass to 25% or less of landscaped area	
2.2.1.3	5	Landscape with plants appropriate for site topography and soil types, emphasizing use of plants with low watering requirements [drought tolerant]	
2.2.1.4	3	Plumb for greywater irrigation	
2.2.1.5	3	Install intelligent irrigation system	
2.2.1.6	2	Sub-surface or drip systems used for irrigation	
2.2.1.7	10	Install landscaping that requires no potable water for irrigation whatsoever after initial establishment period (approximately 1 year)	
2.2.1.8	1--15	Install rainwater collection system (cistern) for reuse	
2.2.1.9	10	Bonus points: No turf grass	
		Subtotal	

Indoor Conservation

2.2.2.1	1	Select bathroom faucets with GPM less than code	
2.2.2.2	1	Select kitchen faucets with GPM less than code	
2.2.2.3	1	Select toilets that meet code, work with the first flush	
2.2.2.4	5	Bonus points: Stub-in plumbing to use greywater water for toilet flushing	
2.2.2.5	10	Bonus points: Use greywater water for toilet flushing	
2.2.2.6	10	Bonus points: Install composting toilets	
2.2.2.7	2--8	Bonus points: Install Dual Flush Toilets	
2.2.2.8	2	Install a recirculating pump for domestic hot water	
		Subtotal	

Eliminate Water Pollutants

2.2.3.1	1	Educate owners/tenants about fish-friendly moss control	
2.2.3.2	3	Provide food waste chutes and compost or worm bins instead of a food garbage disposal	
2.2.3.3	3	Install a whole house water filter system.	
		Subtotal	

DESIGN ALTERNATIVES

2.3.1.1	10	Bonus Points: Provide an accessory dwelling unit or accessory living quarters	
2.3.1.2	1	Bonus Points: Build north area of the lot first, retaining south area for outdoor activities	
2.3.1.3	5	Bonus Points: Provide a front porch	
2.3.1.4	2	Bonus Points: Position garage so it is not in front of house	
2.3.1.5	2--5	Bonus Points: Minimize garage size	
2.3.1.6	4	Bonus Points: Build within ¼ mile of a transit stop	
		Subtotal	
221		**SITE & WATER SECTION TOTALS**	

SECTION THREE: ENERGY EFFICIENCY

ENVELOPE

Thermal Performance

3.1.1.1	10--40	Document envelope improvements beyond code (component performance approach)	
3.1.1.2	1--55	Document envelope improvements beyond code (prescriptive approach)	
3.1.1.3	1	Install rigid insulation beneath any slabs on grade	
3.1.1.4	5	Install dense packed cellulose (over 2.5 lbs/inch) or wet blown cellulose or blown in foam or fiberglass BIBS as insulation	
3.1.1.5	8	Bonus Points: Participate in a program that provides third-party review and inspection	
3.1.1.6	1	Install no more than 1% of floor space of skylights	
3.1.1.7	2	Install a high albedo roof (cool roof)	
3.1.1.8	50	Build a zero net energy home that draws zero outside power or fuel on a net annual basis	
		Subtotal	

Air Sealing

3.1.2.1	3	Airtight Drywall Approach for framed structures	
3.1.2.2	3	Use airtight building method, such as SIP or ICF	
3.1.2.3	5--10	Blower door test results better than .30 ACH (5pts); 0.25 ACH (10pts) [must also complete action item 4.6.1.10]	
		Subtotal	

Reduce Thermal Bridging

3.1.3.1	1	Use insulated headers	
3.1.3.2	1	Fully insulate corners (requires 2-stud instead of 3-stud corners)	
3.1.3.3	1	Fully insulate at interior/exterior wall intersection by open cavity framing (see reference guide)	
3.1.3.4	3	Use energy heels of 6 in. or more on trusses to allow added insulation over top plate	
3.1.3.5	10	Use structural insulated panels on whole house	
3.1.3.6	2	Use insulated exterior sheathing	
3.1.3.7	5	Use advanced wall framing—24-in OC, w/double top plate	
3.1.3.8	5	Innovative stick framing to reduce thermal bridging, by methods such as double wall framing, and horizontal wall furring	
		Subtotal	

Solar Design Features

3.1.4.1	6	Passive solar design, basic features installed	
3.1.4.2	12	Passive solar design, advanced features installed	
3.1.4.3	4--10	Demonstrate a reduction in space conditioning energy, using approved energy modeling software	
3.1.4.4	3	Model solar design features using approved modeling software	
		Subtotal	

Built Green™ Checklist (continued)

HEATING/COOLING				
Distribution				
3.2.1.1	1	Centrally locate heating / cooling system to reduce the size of the distribution system		
3.2.1.2	1	Two properly supported ceiling fan pre-wires		
3.2.1.3	2	Use advanced sealing of all ducts using low toxic mastic		
3.2.1.4	3	Performance test duct for air leakage meets third-party review and certification		
3.2.1.5	5	3rd Party duct test results less than 6% loss of floor area to outside/total flow		
3.2.1.6	5	All ducts are in conditioned space		
3.2.1.7	4	Locate heating / cooling equipment inside the conditioned space		
3.2.1.8	5--10--15	Install hydronic heating systems, point range based on boiler efficiency		
			Subtotal	
Controls				
3.2.2.1	1	Install thermostat with on-switch for furnace fan to circulate air		
3.2.2.2	2	Install 60-minute timers or humidistat for bathroom and laundry room fans		
3.2.2.3	2	Install programmable thermostats		
3.2.2.4	3	Select high efficiency heat pumps instead of electric heat		
			Subtotal	
Heat Recovery				
3.2.3.1	3--4	Install a heat recovery ventilator or an energy recovery ventilator		
			Subtotal	
Heating/Cooling				
3.2.4.1	3	Select Energy Star® heating / cooling equipment		
3.2.4.2	2	No gas fireplaces, use direct vent gas or propane hearth product (AFUE rating)		
3.2.4.3	5	No air conditioner		
3.2.4.4	3	Install on-demand water heating used for space heating		
3.2.4.5	10	Install geothermal heat pumps		
			Subtotal	
WATER HEATING				
Distribution				
3.3.1.1	2	Locate water heater within 20 pipe feet of highest use		
3.3.1.2	1	Insulate all hot water pipes and install cold inlet heat traps on hot water heater		
			Subtotal	
Drain water Heat Recovery				
3.3.2.1	2	Install drainwater heat recovery system (DHR)		
			Subtotal	
Water Heating				
3.3.3.1	2	Passive or on-demand hot water delivery system installed at farthest location from water heater		
3.3.3.2	2	Install tankless hot water heater		
3.3.3.3	2--7	Upgrade gas or propane water heater efficiency to 0.61, 0.83, or .90		
3.3.3.4	2	Install the water heater inside the heated space (electric, direct vent, or sealed venting only)		
3.3.3.5	4	Upgrade electric water heater to exhaust air heat pump water heater or de-superheater: EF 1.9		
3.3.3.6	3	Install a timer to regulate standby hot water loss in hot water heater.		
3.3.3.7	3	Install instant hot water systems (where appropriate)		
			Subtotal	
LIGHTING				
Natural Light				
3.4.1.1	1	Light-colored interior finishes		
3.4.1.2	2	Use clerestory for natural lighting		
3.4.1.3	2	Use light tubes for natural lighting and to reduce electric lighting		
			Subtotal	
Solar Powered Lighting				
3.4.2.1	1	Solar-powered walkway or outdoor area lighting		
			Subtotal	
Efficient Lighting				
3.4.3.1	1	Furnish four compact fluorescent light bulbs to owners (req'd if installing screw-in compacts, See Action Item 3.4.3.5)		
3.4.3.2	1	Halogen lighting substituted for incandescent down-lights		
3.4.3.3	3	Install lighting dimmer, photo cells, timers, and/or motion detectors (interior)		
3.4.3.4	2	Install photo cells, timers, motion detectors (exterior)		
3.4.3.5	2--5	Use compact fluorescent bulbs, ballast, or fixtures in three high-use locations (kitchen, porch/outdoors, and one other location)		
3.4.3.6	1	Use air lock can lights instead of IC rated		
3.4.3.7	1--10	Install hard-wired fluorescent fixtures, with 1 point for each 10% of lighting		
3.4.3.8	1	Hard Wired fluorescents on dimmer		
3.4.3.9	1	Install LED lighting		
			Subtotal	

Built Green™ Checklist (continued)

APPLIANCES

3.5.1.1	1	Provide an outdoor clothesline	
3.5.1.2	1	Install gas clothes dryer	
3.5.1.3	3	Install a front loading or Energy Star® washing machine	
3.5.1.4	1	Install an Energy Star® dishwasher	
3.5.1.5	2	Install Energy Star® refrigerator	
3.5.1.6	2	Install Gas Stove/Cooktop (requires a carbon monoxide detector)	
3.5.1.7	2	Install biofuel appliances	
3.5.1.8	2	Install Energy Star® exhaust fans	
		Subtotal	

EFFICIENT DESIGN

3.6.1.1	2	Use building and landscaping plans that reduce heating/cooling loads naturally	
3.6.1.2	5	Install heat systems with separate zones for sleeping and living areas	
		Subtotal	

ALTERNATIVE ENERGY (Bonus Points)

3.7.1.1	2--3	Enroll the residence in the local utility's electricity program for renewable electricity sources	
3.7.1.2	10	Solar water heating system sized to provide a minimum of 40% hot water designed energy use	
3.7.1.3	2	Pre-pipe for Solar Water Heater	
3.7.1.4	5--25	Bonus Points: House powered by photovoltaic	
3.7.1.5	5--25	Install innovative non-solar renewable power systems that produce a minimum of 15%, 30%, or 50% of the houses total annual energy	
		Subtotal	
241		**ENERGY EFFICIENCY SECTION TOTALS**	

SECTION 4: HEALTH AND INDOOR AIR QUALITY

OVERALL

4.1.1.1	5	Assist homeowners with chemical sensitivities to identify preferred IAQ measures and finishes	
4.1.1.2	5	Project team member to have taken American Lung Association (ALA) of Washington "Healthy House Professional Training" course or other IAQ class with 8 hours of curriculum minimum.	
4.1.1.3	15	Certify house under EPA IAQ Star Program, ALA Health House Program, or other program as approved by the Director.	
4.1.1.4	2	Provide homeowners with maintenance checklists (furnace filters, under the fridge, etc…)	
		Subtotal	

JOB-SITE OPERATIONS

4.2.1.1	1	Use less-toxic cleaners	
4.2.1.2	1	Require workers to use VOC-safe masks when applying VOC containing wet products, and N-95 dust masks when generating dust	
4.2.1.3	3--5	Take measures during construction operations to avoid moisture problems later (see Handbook for Basic and Expanded levels)	
4.2.1.4	2	Take measures to avoid problems due to construction dust by doing all bullets in the handbook	
4.2.1.5	3	Ventilate with box fans in windows blowing out during drywall sanding and new wet finish applications	
4.2.1.6	2	No use of unvented heaters during construction	
4.2.1.7	3	Clean duct and furnace thoroughly just before owners move in	
4.2.1.8	4	Train subs in implementing a healthy building job-site plan for the project	
		Subtotal	

LAYOUT AND MATERIAL SELECTION

4.3.1.1	1	Use prefinished flooring	
4.3.1.2	2	If using carpet, specify CRI Green Label Plus or Greenguard or equivalent as approved by the Director.	
4.3.1.3	1	Do not install either insulation or carpet padding with brominated flame retardant in them.	
4.3.1.4	1	Install low pile or less allergen-attracting carpet and pad	
4.3.1.5	3	Limit use of carpet to one-third of home's square footage	
4.3.1.6	2--6	Optimize air quality in family bedrooms to basic or advanced level as per completing items listed in handbook	
4.3.1.7	1	If using carpet, install by dry method	
4.3.1.8	5	Detached or no garage OR garage air-sealed from house with automatic exhaust fan	
4.3.1.9	3	Use urea formaldehyde-free insulation or Greenguard certified product	
4.3.1.10	4	Do not use fiberglass insulation	
4.3.1.11		Inside the home, use only low-VOC, low-toxic, water-based, solvent-free sealers, grouts, mortars, drywall mud, caulks, adhesives, stains, pigments and additives for:	
4.3.1.12	2	Tile and Grout	
4.3.1.13	2	Framing	
4.3.1.14	4	Flooring	
4.3.1.15	2	Plumbing	
4.3.1.16	2	HVAC	
4.3.1.17	2	Insulation	
4.3.1.18	2	Drywall	
4.3.1.19	3	Use plywood and composites of exterior grade or with no added urea formaldehyde (for interior use)	
4.3.1.20	5	Install cabinets with no added urea formaldehyde board and low-toxic finish	
4.3.1.21	3	Use ceramic tile for 5% of flooring	
4.3.1.22	5	Use only shelving, window trim, door trim, base molding etc., with no added urea formaldehyde.	
4.3.1.23	3	Use no PVC piping for plumbing	
4.3.1.24	1	Install natural fiber carpet (e.g. wool)	
4.3.1.25	3	Use only low-VOC /low-toxic interior paints and finishes for large surface areas	
4.3.1.26	5	Use only low-VOC/low toxic interior paints and finishes for all surface areas (including doors, windows, trim)	
4.3.1.27	1	Use only paints and finishes without cadmium or lead.	
4.3.1.28	15	No carpet	
		Subtotal	

Built Green™ Checklist (continued)

MOISTURE CONTROL			
4.4.1.1	1	Grade to drain away from buildings	
4.4.1.2	1	Verify seal at doors, windows, plumbing and electrical penetrations against moisture and air leaks	
4.4.1.3	3	Envelope inspection at pre-insulation by a qualified professional	
4.4.1.4	2	Slab on grade, upgrade under slab moisture barrier beyond code to 10mil minimum; minimum of 10mil poly in crawl spaces with sealed seams and sealed perimeter	
4.4.1.5	1	Use ridge vents for venting attic	
4.4.1.6	1	Prepare a roof water management plan showing best practices for the site soils and storm water infrastructure	
4.4.1.7	3	Roof overhangs are at least 24"	
4.4.1.8	2	Protect windows and doors on tall walls with additional overhang protection	
4.4.1.9	6	Install a drain plane for walls between siding, trim & building paper or house wrap	
4.4.1.10		Install:	
4.4.1.11	7	a sloped sill pan with end dams and back dams for all windows, and back dams for all exterior doors exposed to the weather	
4.4.1.12	3	back dams or sloped sill at all window sills	
4.4.1.13	1	Install metal flashing at all windows	
4.4.1.14	1	Install metal flashing at door heads exposed to the weather	
4.4.1.15	3	Hose test first installed window to verify resistance to wind driven rain	
4.4.1.16	2	Install working "radon" type vent system to eliminate potential moisture, methane, and radon problems in crawl space or under slabs on grade	
4.4.1.17	1	Install a rigid perforated footing drain at foundation perimeter, not connected to roof drain system.	
4.4.1.18	3	Show & build moisture management details for below grade walls beyond code, such as dimple drainage mat at exterior face, and capillary breaks.	
4.4.1.19	2	Perform calcium chloride moisture test on all slabs on grade prior to installing any finish flooring in conformance with product warranties.	
4.4.1.20	3	Have crawl space, attic and garage building performance tested for disconnection to the living space of house.	
		Subtotal	
AIR DISTRIBUTION AND FILTRATION			
4.5.1.1	2	Do not install electronic, metal mesh, horse hair, or non-pleated fiberglass filters	
4.5.1.2		Use effective air filter:	
4.5.1.3	1	Use medium efficiency pleated filter, MERV 10	
4.5.1.4	5	Use high efficiency pleated filter, MERV 12 or better, or HEPA	
4.5.1.5	2	Balance airflow system based on filter being used	
4.5.1.6	3	Install central vacuum, exhausted to outside	
4.5.1.7	2	Provide for cross ventilation using operable windows	
		Subtotal	
HVAC EQUIPMENT			
4.6.1.1	1	Flow test all fans in the house	
4.6.1.2	1	Use heating system controls that are free of mercury	
4.6.1.3	1	Limit kitchen exhaust fan to 300 cfm maximum	
4.6.1.4	1	Install 60-minute timer switches for bath exhaust fans or HRV override switch.	
4.6.1.5	2	Install quiet (<1.5 sone) bath fan with smooth ducting, minimum 4 in. or employ other quiet ventilation strategy.	
4.6.1.6	1	Install exhaust fans in rooms where office equipment is used	
4.6.1.7	3	Install sealed combustion heating and hot water equipment	
4.6.1.8	3	Install power venting for combustion furnaces and water heating equipment (cannot be taken in addition to 4.6.1.7)	
4.6.1.9	3	Install exhaust fan in attached garage on timer or wired to door opener, or no garage attached to house	
4.6.1.10	2	Install whole house fan beyond the code requirements	
4.6.1.11	1	No sound insulation or other fibrous materials installed inside ducting	
4.6.1.12	5	Bonus Points: Provide balanced or slightly positive indoor pressure using controlled ventilation	
4.6.1.13	3	Install timer control integrated with thermostat on whole house ventilation system with balanced or positive pressure, or continually running HRV.	
4.6.1.14	10	Install whole house radiant heating system (No ducted heating)	
		Subtotal	
HEALTH & INDOOR AIR QUALITY			
4.7.1.1	1	Build a lockable storage closet for hazardous cleaning & maintenance products, separate from occupied space	
4.7.1.2	1	If installing water filter at sink, select one with biodegradable carbon filter	
4.7.1.3	1	Install showerhead filter	
4.7.1.4	3	Do not install a wood-burning fireplace inside house	
4.7.1.5	1	Do not install gas-burning appliances inside house	
4.7.1.6	3	Design a shoe removal vestibule at major entrances to house (front, back, garage)	
4.7.1.7	1--2	Install floor drain or catch basin with drain under washing machine and/or water heater.	
4.7.1.8	1	Install moisture alarms under sinks and dishwasher	
		Subtotal	
223		HEALTH AND INDOOR AIR QUALITY SECTION TOTALS	

Built Green™ Checklist (continued)

SECTION FIVE: MATERIALS EFFICIENCY			
OVERALL			
5.1.1.1	10	Enroll project in King County *Construction Works* Program OR in Snohomish County, meets equivalent criteria	
5.1.1.2	5--9	Design and build for deconstruction concept	
5.1.1.3	1--5	Eliminate materials & systems that require finishes on a minimum of 100 square feet	
5.1.1.4	2--6	Use of domestic agriculturally based oil products in insulation, piping, or finishes as an alternative to petroleum	
JOBSITE OPERATIONS			
5.2.1.1	1	Provide weather protection for stored materials	
5.2.1.2	1	Substitute products that require solvent-based cleaning methods with solvent-free or water-based methods.	
		Subtotal	
Reduce			
5.2.2.1	2	Create detailed take-off and provide as cut list to framer	
5.2.2.2	2	Use central cutting area or cut packs	
5.2.2.3	2	Require subcontractors and contractor's employees to participate in waste reduction efforts	
		Subtotal	
Reuse			
5.2.3.1	2--20	Use deconstruction to dismantle and reuse existing building(s) on site	
5.2.3.2	1	Sell or give away wood scraps, lumber and land clearing debris	
5.2.3.3	1	Donate, give away, or sell reusable finish items	
5.2.3.4	1	Re-use doors	
5.2.3.5	1	Re-use flooring	
5.2.3.6	1	Re-use windows	
5.2.3.7	1	Re-use appliances	
5.2.3.8	1	Re-use fixtures	
5.2.3.9	1	Re-use hardware	
5.2.3.10	1	Re-use cabinets	
5.2.3.11	1	Re-use siding	
5.2.3.12	1	Re-use decking	
5.2.3.13	1	Re-use trim	
5.2.3.14	1	Re-use framing lumber	
		Subtotal	
Recycle			
Source Separation Recycling			
5.2.4.1	1	Recycle cardboard by source separation, 85% minimum recycling rate.	
5.2.4.2	2	Recycle metal scraps by source separation, 85% minimum recycling rate.	
5.2.4.3	5	Recycle clean scrap wood and broken pallets by source separation, 85% minimum recycling rate.	
5.2.4.4	2	Recycle plastic wrap and pallet wrap by source separation, 85% minimum recycling rate.	
5.2.4.5	3	Recycle drywall by source separation, 85% minimum recycling rate.	
5.2.4.6	2	Recycle concrete/asphalt rubble, masonry materials, or porcelain by source separation, 85% minimum recycling rate.	
5.2.4.7	1	Recycle paint by source separation, 85% minimum recycling rate.	
5.2.4.8	4	Recycle asphalt roofing by source separation, 85% minimum recycling rate.	
5.2.4.9	2	Recycle carpet padding and upholstery foam by source separation, 85% minimum recycling rate.	
5.2.4.10	1	Recycle glass by source separation, 85% minimum recycling rate	
5.2.4.11	3	Recycle land clearing and yard waste, soil and sod by source separation, 85% minimum recycling rate.	
Co-mingle Recycle			
5.2.5.1	10	At least 85% of jobsite waste(by weight excluding concrete) is sent to a co-mingled recycling facility with 60% recycling rate	
5.2.5.2	18	At least 85% of jobsite waste (by weight excluding concrete) is sent to a co-mingled recycling facility with 75% recycling rate	
5.2.5.3	24	At least 85% of jobsite waste (by weight excluding concrete) is sent to a co-mingled recycling facility with 90% recycling rate	
5.2.5.4	4	Commingle recycle at least 50% of jobsite debris, and take to a facility with a minimum recycling rate of 50%.	
5.2.5.5	3--12	Bonus Points for overall recycling rate above 50%, 70% or 90% by weight.	
		Subtotal	
DESIGN AND MATERIAL SELECTION			
Overall			
5.3.1.1	1	Use standard dimensions in design of structure	
5.3.1.2	1	Install materials with longer life cycles	
5.3.1.3	1--3	Install locally produced materials	
5.3.1.4	1--8	Use building salvaged lumber, minimum 500 board feet.	
5.3.1.5	2--3	Use urban or forest salvaged lumber, minimum 250 board feet.	
5.3.1.6	1	Use any amount of rapidly renewable building materials and products made from plants harvested within a ten-year cycle or shorter	
5.3.1.7	3	In three applications, use rapidly renewable building materials and products made from plants harvested within a ten-year cycle or shorter	
5.3.1.8	1--10	Bonus points for re-use of salvaged materials	
5.3.1.9	3	Use no endangered wood species	
5.3.1.10	2	Use environmentally preferable products with third-party certifications such as SCS, Floor Score, and Green Seal. (Not applicable to carpet)	
		Subtotal	

Built Green™ Checklist (continued)

Framing		
5.3.2.1	7	Use dimensional lumber that is third party certified sustainably harvested wood, 50% minimum. Tier 1 - See Built Green Handboo
5.3.2.2	3	Use dimensional lumber that is third party certified sustainably harvested wood, 50% minimum. Tier 2 - See Built Green Handboo
5.3.2.3	5	Use sheathing that is third party certified sustainably harvested wood, 50% minimum. Tier 1 - See Built Green Handbook
5.3.2.4	2	Use sheathing that is third party certified sustainably harvested wood, 50% minimum. Tier 2 - See Built Green Handbook
5.3.2.5	5	Use beams that are third party certified sustainably harvested wood, 50% minimum. Tier 1 - See Built Green Handbook
5.3.2.6	2	Use beams that are third party certified sustainably harvested wood, 50% minimum. Tier 2 - See Built Green Handbook
5.3.2.7	1	Use factory framed wall panels (panelized wall construction)
5.3.2.8	3	Use engineered structural products and use no dimensional 2xs larger than 2x8, and no 4xs larger than 4x8
5.3.2.9	4	Use structural insulated panels
5.3.2.10	3	Use insulated concrete forms
5.3.2.11	2--3	Use finger-jointed studs
5.3.2.12	5	Use advanced system framing with double top plate
		Subtotal

Foundation		
5.3.3.1	1	Use regionally produced block
5.3.3.2	6	Use flyash or blast furnace slag for 25% by weight of cementitious materials for all concrete (20% for flat work)
5.3.3.3	2	Use recycled concrete, asphalt, or glass cullet for base or fill
		Subtotal

Sub-Floor		
5.3.4.1	1	Use recycled-content sub-floor
		Subtotal

Doors		
5.3.5.1	2	Use domestically-grown wood interior doors
		Subtotal

Finish Floor		
5.3.6.1	4	No vinyl flooring
5.3.6.2	1	Use any amount of rapidly renewable flooring products with a ten-year harvest cycle or shorter (excluding carpet)
5.3.6.3	3	On more than 250 square feet, use rapidly renewable flooring with a ten-year harvest cycle or shorter (excluding carpet)
5.3.6.4	1	Use recycled-content carpet pad
5.3.6.5	1	Use recycled-content or renewed carpet
5.3.6.6	1	Use replaceable carpet tile
5.3.6.7	3	Use 40% recycled content hard surface tile, 100 square feet minimum
5.3.6.8	3	Use natural linoleum
5.3.6.9	1--5	Use locally salvaged wood flooring
5.3.6.10	5	Use flooring that is third party certified sustainably harvested wood, 50% minimum. Tier 1 - See Built Green Handbook
5.3.6.11	2	Use flooring that is third party certified sustainably harvested wood, 50% minimum. Tier 2 - See Built Green Handbook
5.3.6.12	1	Use durable/spot repairable floor finish
5.3.6.13	2	Use concrete slab or sub-floor as a finished floor in living space.
		Subtotal

Interior Walls		
5.3.7.1	4	Use drywall with a minimum of 90% recycled-content gypsum or flue gas substitute for recycled gypsum
5.3.7.2	2	Use recycled or "reworked" paint and finishes
5.3.7.3	1	Use recycled newspaper or cork expansion joint filler
5.3.7.4	1--3	Use natural wall finishes, like lime paint and clay
5.3.7.5	2	Reduce interior walls, through open plan for kitchen, dining & living areas.
		Subtotal

Exterior Walls		
5.3.8.1	3	Use siding with reclaimed or recycled material on at least 20% of solid wall surface
5.3.8.2	4	No vinyl siding or exterior trim
5.3.8.3	2	Use 50-year siding product
5.3.8.4	5	Use wood siding that is third party certified sustainably harvested wood on at least 20% of solid wall surface. Tier 1 - See Built Green Handbook
5.3.8.5	2	Use wood siding that is third party certified sustainably harvested wood on at least 20% of solid wall surface. Tier 2 - See Built Green Handbook
5.3.8.6	3	Use salvaged masonry brick or block, 50% minimum
5.3.8.7	2	Use regionally produced stone or brick
5.3.8.8	5	Use straw bale walls, minimum R-28
		Subtotal

Windows		
5.3.9.1	3	Use wood or composite or fiberglass windows
5.3.9.2	4	No vinyl windows.
5.3.9.3	1	Use finger-jointed wood windows
5.3.9.4	5	Use wood windows that are third party certified sustainably harvested wood. Tier 1 - See Built Green Handbook
5.3.9.5	2	Use wood windows that are third party certified sustainably harvested wood. Tier 2 - See Built Green Handbook
		Subtotal

Built Green™ Checklist (continued)

Cabinetry and Trim			
5.3.10.1		If using trim:	
5.3.10.2	1	Use regional products, 50% minimum	
5.3.10.3	3	Use trim that is third party certified sustainably harvested wood, 50% minimum. Tier 1 - See Built Green	
5.3.10.4	1	Use trim that is third party certified sustainably harvested, 50% minimum. Tier 2 - See Built Green Handbook	
5.3.10.5	3	Use finger-jointed trim, MDF trim with no added urea formaldehyde, or wood alternative with no added urea formaldehyde, 90% minimum	
5.3.10.6	1	Use wood veneers that are third party certified sustainably harvested wood, 50% minimum. Tier 1 - See Built Green Handbook.	
5.3.10.7		For cabinets:	
5.3.10.8	2	Use regional products, 90% minimum	
5.3.10.9	3	Use wood that is third party certified sustainably harvested wood, 50% minimum. Tier 1 - See Built Green	
5.3.10.10	1	Handbook	
5.3.10.11	2--3	Use cabinet casework and shelving constructed of agricultural fiber ("strawboard" or "wheatboard") with no added urea formaldehyde	
5.3.10.12	1	Use countertops that are salvaged, recycled, or third party certified sustainably harvested wood as Tier 1 in the Built Green Handbook	
		Subtotal	
Roof			
5.3.11.1	2	Use recycled-content roofing material	
5.3.11.2	2	Use 30-year warranted roofing material	
5.3.11.3	3	Use 40-year warranted roofing material	
5.3.11.4	2	Use Solar shingles	
5.3.11.5	3	Install a metal roof	
		Subtotal	
Insulation			
5.3.12.1	2	All insulation to have a minimum of 40% recycled content	
5.3.12.2	3	Use environmentally friendly foam building products (formaldehyde-free, CFC-free, HCFC-free)	
		Subtotal	
Other Exterior			
5.3.13.1	2	Use reclaimed or salvaged material for landscaping walls	
5.3.13.2	3	Use 100% recycled content HDPE, salvaged lumber, or lumber that is third party certified sustainably harvested wood at the Tier 1 level (see Built Green Handbook) for decking and porches	
5.3.13.3	4	Bonus points: Use no pressure treated lumber	
5.3.13.4	5+	Points for B20 biodiesel or better equipment (5 points for 100% excavation equipment on biodiesel, 1 point for any additional vehicle frequently on site)	
		Subtotal	
RECYCLING			
5.4.1.1	2	Provide built-in kitchen or utility room recycling center	
		Subtotal	
	238	MATERIALS EFFICIENCY SECTION TOTALS	
EXTRA CREDIT			
EC 1	1--10	Extra credit for innovation	
		Subtotal	
	0	EXTRA CREDIT TOTALS	
	923	Project Scoring Sub-Total	
		(Action Item 5-3) Multiplier	
		PROJECT SCORING TOTAL	
		PROJECT SUMMARIES	
		CODES & REGULATIONS	X
		SITE & WATER SECTION TOTALS	
		ENERGY EFFICIENCY SECTION TOTALS	
		HEALTH AND INDOOR AIR QUALITY SECTION TOTALS	
		MATERIALS EFFICIENCY SECTION TOTALS	

Project Checklist
LEED for Homes

Builder Name:
Home Address (Street/City/State):

Input Values:
No of Bedrooms: **4** Floor Area (SF): **2400**

Minimum No. of Points Required:
Certified: **45** Silver: **60** Gold: **75** Platinum: **90**

Detailed information on the measures below are provided in the companion document "LEED for Homes Rating System"

Max Points Available

Innovation and Design Process (ID) — (Minimum of 0 ID Points Required) — 9

Y/Pts	No	N/A	#	Measure	Description		Max Points
			1.1	Integrated Project Planning	Preliminary Rating		Prerequisite
		☜	1.2		Integrated Project Team		1
		☜	1.3		Design Charrette		1
		☜	2.1	Quality Management for	Durability Planning; (Pre-Construction)		Prerequisite
			2.2	Durability	Wet Room Measures		Prerequisite
			2.3		Quality Management		Prerequisite
			2.4		Third-Party Durability Inspection		3
		☜	3.1	Innovative / Regional Design	Provide Description and Justification for Specific Measure		1
		☜	3.2		Provide Description and Justification for Specific Measure		1
		☜	3.3		Provide Description and Justification for Specific Measure		1
		☜	3.4		Provide Description and Justification for Specific Measure		1
0				Sub-Total			

Location and Linkages (LL) — (Minimum of 0 LL Points Required) — OR — 10

Y/Pts	No	N/A	#	Measure	Description		Max Points
			1	LEED-ND Neighborhood		LL2-5	10
		☜	2	Site Selection	Avoid Environmentally Sensitive Sites and Farmland	LL1	2
			3.1	Preferred Locations	Select an Edge Development Site	LL1	1
			3.2		OR Select an Infill Site	LL1	2
			3.3		Select a Previously Developed Site	LL1	1
			4	Infrastructure	Site within 1/2 Mile of Existing Water and Sewer	LL1	1
			5.1	Community Resources	Basic Community Resources / Public Transportation	LL1	1
			5.2	& Public Transit	OR Extensive Community Resources / Public Transportation	LL1	2
			5.3		OR Outstanding Community Resources / Public Transportation	LL1	3
			6	Access to Open Space	Publicly Accessible Green Spaces	LL1	1
0				Sub-Total			

Sustainable Sites (SS) — (Minimum of 5 SS Points Required) — OR — 21

Y/Pts	No	N/A	#	Measure	Description		Max Points
			1.1	Site Stewardship	Erosion Controls (During Construction)		Prerequisite
			1.2		Minimize Disturbed Area of Site		1
		☜	2.1	Landscaping	No Invasive Plants		Prerequisite
		☜	2.2		Basic Landscaping Design		2
		☜	2.3		Limit Turf		3
		☜	2.4		Drought Tolerant Plants		2
		☜	3	Shading of Hardscapes	Locate and Plant Trees to Shade Hardscapes		1
		☜	4.1	Surface Water Management	Design Permeable Site		4
			4.2		Design and Install Permanent Erosion Controls		2
			5	Non-Toxic Pest Contro	Select Insect and Pest Control Alternatives from List		2
		☜	6.1	Compact Development	Average Housing Density≥ 7 Units / Acre	LL1	2
		☜	6.1		OR Average Housing Density≥ 10 Units / Acre	LL1	3
		☜	6.3		OR Average Housing Density≥ 20 Units / Acre	LL1	4
0				Sub-Total			

Water Efficiency (WE) — (Minimum of 3 WE Points Required) — OR — 15

Y/Pts	No	N/A	#	Measure	Description		Max Points
		☜	1.1	Water Reuse	Rainwater Harvesting System		4
		☜	1.2		Grey Water Re-Use System		1
		☜	2.1	Irrigation System	Select High Efficiency Measures from List		3
			2.2		Third Party Verification		1
		☜	2.3		OR Install Landscape Designed by Licensed or Certified Professional	WE 2.2	4
			3.1	Indoor Water Use	High Efficiency Fixtures (Toilets, Showers, and Faucets)		3
			3.2		OR Very High Efficiency Fixtures (Toilets, Showers, and Faucets)	WE 3.1	6
0				Sub-Total			

Project Checklist (cont'd)

HERS Index Value Achieved: 86   IECC Climate Zone: 1   EA 1.2 Pts Achieved: 0.0

Y / Pts	No	N/A					
			Energy and Atmosphere (EA)		(Minimum of 0 EA Points Required)	OR	**38**
			1.1 **ENERGY STAR Home**	Meets ENERGY STAR for Homes with Third-Party Testing			Prerequisite
			1.2	Exceeds ENERGY STAR for Homes		EA 2-10	34
		⊠	7.1 **Water Heating**	Improved Hot Water Distribution System			2
			7.2	Pipe Insulation			1
		⊠	11 **Refrigerant Management**	Minimize Ozone Depletion and Global Warming Contribution			1
0			Sub-Total (or Sub-Total from Adendum A - Prescriptive EA Credits)				
			Materials and Resources (MR)		(Minimum of 2 MR Points Required)		**14**
		⊠	1.1 **Material Efficient Framing**	Overall Waste Factor for Framing Order Shall be No More than 10%.			Prerequisite
			1.2	Advanced Framing Techniques			3
			1.3	OR Structurally Insulated Panels		MR 1.2	2
		⊠	2.1 **Environmentally Preferable**	Tropical Woods, if Used, Must be FSC			Prerequisite
		⊠	2.2 **Products**	Select Environmentally Preferable Products from List			8
		⊠	3.1 **Waste Management**	Document Overall Rate of Diversion			Prerequisite
			3.2	Reduce Waste Sent to Landfill by 25% to 100%			3
0			Sub-Total				
			Indoor Environmental Quality (IEQ)		(Minimum of 6 IEQ Points Required)	OR	**20**
			1 **ENERGY STAR with IAP**	Meets ENERGY STAR w/ Indoor Air Package (IAP)		IEQ2-10	11
			2.1 **Combustion Venting**	Space Heating & DHW Equip w/ Closed/Power-Exhaust		IEQ 1	Prerequisite
			2.2	Install High Performance Fireplace		IEQ 1	2
		⊠	3 **Moisture Control**	Analyze Moisture Loads AND Install Central System (if Needed)		IEQ 1	1
		⊠	4.1 **Outdoor Air Ventilation**	Meets ASHRAE Std 62.2		IEQ 1	Prerequisite
			4.2	Dedicated Outdoor Air System (w/ Heat Recovery)		IEQ 1	2
			4.3	Third-Party Testing of Outdoor Air Flow Rate into Home			1
		⊠	5.1 **Local Exhaust**	Meets ASHRAE Std 62.2		IEQ 1	Prerequisite
			5.2	Timer / Automatic Controls for Bathroom Exhaust Fans		IEQ 1	1
			5.3	Third-Party Testing of Exhaust Air Flow Rate Out of Home			1
		⊠	6.1 **Supply Air Distribution**	Meets ACCA Manual D		IEQ 1	Prerequisite
			6.2	Third-Party Testing of Supply Air Flow into Each Room in Home			2
			7.1 **Supply Air Filtering**	≥ 8 MERV Filters, w/ Adequate System Air Flow		IEQ 1	Prerequisite
			7.2	OR ≥ 10 MERV Filters, w/ Adequate System Air Flow			1
			7.3	OR ≥ 13 MERV Filters, w/ Adequate System Air Flow			2
			8.1 **Contaminant Control**	Seal-Off Ducts During Construction		IEQ 1	1
			8.2	Permanent Walk-Off Mats OR Shoe Storage OR Central Vacuum			2
		⊠	8.3	Flush Home Continuously for 1 Week with Windows Open			1
		⊠	9.1 **Radon Protection**	Install Radon Resistant Construction if Home is in EPA Zone 1		IEQ 1	Prerequisite
		⊠	9.2	Install Radon Resistant Construction if Home is not in EPA Zone 1		IEQ 1	1
			10.1 **Garage Pollutant Protection**	No Air Handling Equipment OR Return Ducts in Garage		IEQ 1	Prerequisite
			10.2	Tightly Seal Shared Surfaces between Garage and Home		IEQ 1	2
			10.3	Exhaust Fan in Garage			1
			10.4	OR Detached Garage or No Garage		IEQ 1	3
0			Sub-Total				
			Awareness and Education (AE)		(Minimum of 0 AE Points Required)		**3**
		⊠	1.1 **Education for Homeowner**	Basic Occupant's Manual and Walkthrough of LEED Home			Prerequisite
		⊠	1.2 **and/or Tenants**	Comprehensive Occupant's Manual and Multiple Walkthroughs / Trainings			1
		⊠	1.3	Public Awareness of LEED Home			1
		⊠	2.1 **Education for Building Mgrs**	Basic Building Manager's Manual and Walkthrough of LEED Home			1
0			Sub-Total				
0			**Project Totals (pre-certification estimates)**		*Estimated Performance Tier:*		**130**

for Homes

Project Checklist, Addendum A
Prescriptive Approach for Energy and Atmosphere (EA) Credits

Detailed information on the measures below are provided in the companion document "LEED for Homes Rating System"						**Max Points** Available
Y / Pts No N/A		**Energy and Atmosphere (EA)**	(Minimum of 0 EA Points Required)	**OR**	**38**	
		2.1 **Insulation**	Third-Party Inspection of Insulation, At Least HERS Grade II	EA 1	Prerequisite	
	☒	2.2	Third-Party Inspection of Insulation, Grade I AND 5% above code	EA 1	2	
		3.1 **Air Infiltration**	Third-Party Envelope Air Leakage Tested </= 7.0 ACH50 (CZ 1-2)	EA 1	Prerequisite	
		3.2	Third-Party Envelope Air Leakage Tested </= 5.0 ACH50 (CZ 1-2)	EA 1	2	
		3.3	OR Third-Party Envelope Air Leakage Tested </= 3.0 ACH50	EA 1	3	
		4.1 **Windows**	Windows Meet ENERGY STAR for Windows (See Table)	EA 1	Prerequisite	
		4.2	Windows Exceed ENERGY STAR for Windows (See Table)	EA 1	2	
		4.3	OR Windows Exceed ENERGY STAR for Windows (See Table)	EA 1	3	
		5.1 **Duct Tightness**	Third-Party Duct Leakage Tested </= 4.0 CFM25 / 100 SF to Outside	EA 1	Prerequisite	
		5.2	Third-Party Duct Leakage Tested </= 3.0 CFM25 / 100 SF to Outside	EA 1	2	
		5.3	OR Third-Party Duct Leakage Tested </= 1.0 CFM25 / 100 SF to Outside	EA 1	3	
	☒	6.1 **Space Heating and Cooling**	Meets ENERGY STAR for HVAC w/ Manual J & refrigerant charge test	EA 1	Prerequisite	
		6.2	HVAC is Better than ENERGY STAR	EA 1	2	
		6.3	OR HVAC Substantially Exceeds ENERGY STAR	EA 1	4	
	☒	7.1 **Water Heating**	Improved Hot Water Distribution System		2	
		7.2	Pipe Insulation		1	
		7.3 **Water Heating**	Improved Water Heating Equipment	EA 1	3	
		8.1 **Lighting**	Install at Least Three ENERGY STAR labeled Light Fixtures (or CFLS)	EA 1	Prerequisite	
		8.2	Energy Efficient Fixtures and Controls	EA 1	2	
	☒	8.3	OR ENERGY STAR Advanced Lighting Package	EA 1	3	
		9.1 **Appliances**	Select Appliances from List	EA 1	2	
		9.2	Very Efficient Clothes Washer (MEF > 1.8, AND WF< 5.5)	EA 1	1	
	☒	10 **Renewable Energy**	Renewable Electric Generation System (1 Point / 5% Reduction	EA 1	10	
	☒	11 **Refrigerant Management**	Minimize Ozone Depletion and Global Warming Contribution		1	
0		Sub-Total				

By affixing my signature below, the undersigned does hereby declare and affirm to the USGBC that the LEED for Homes requirements, as specified in the LEED for Homes Rating System, have been met for the indicated credits and will, if audited, provide the necessary supporting documents. The undersigned also acknowledges that the builder is solely responsible for choosing LEED for Homes features that are appropriate for the home and for their proper installation. USGBC and its representatives are responsible only for verifying the completion of LEED for Homes requirements as set forth in the LEED for Homes Rating System; such verification in no way constitutes a warranty as to the appropriateness of the selected LEED for Homes measures or the quality of implementation.

Builder's Name		Company	
Signature		Date	

By affixing my signature below, the undersigned does hereby declare and affirm to the USGBC that the required durability plan, accountability forms, inspections, and performance testing for the LEED for Homes requirements, as specified in the LEED for Homes Rating System, have been completed, and will provide the project documentation file, if requested.

Rater's Name		Company	
Signature		Date	

By affixing my signature below, the undersigned does hereby declare and affirm to the USGBC that the required durability plan, accountability forms, inspections, and performance testing for the LEED for Homes requirements, as specified in the LEED for Homes Rating System, have been completed, and will provide the project documentation file, if requested.

Provider's Name		Company	
Signature		Date	